THE EXPANSION MANDATE

The Expansion Mandate Copyright © 2023 Rachel Wortman

All rights reserved.

No part of this publication may be reproduced, stored or transmitted in any form or by any means, electronic, mechanical, photocopying, recording, scanning, or otherwise without written permission from the publisher. It is illegal to copy this book, post it to a website, or distribute it by any other means without permission.

Holy Bible, New International Version®, NIV®. Copyright © 1973, 1978, 1984, 2011 by Biblica Inc.® Used by permission. All rights reserved worldwide. The Amplified Bible (AMP). Copyright © 2015 by The Lockman Foundation, La Habra, CA 90631. All rights reserved.

First edition
Paperback ISBN: 978-1-7340994-8-5

THE EXPANSION MANDATE

The four battles to win on the

journey to your promise land

RACHEL WORTMAN

To Grant, my expansion partner.

This book would not exist without your incredible support and leadership. I will never forget when God told me to marry you because, with you, all my dreams could come true.

You are the picture of an expanded life FULL of fulfilled promises. Your faith inspires me. Your character refines me. Your love empowers me. I love you.

CONTENTS

INTRODUCTION..9

1. THE EXPANSION MANDATE..13

2. BLESSED! A THOUSAND TIMES, BLESSED............................29

3. THE BATTLE *FOR* YOUR PROMISE...39

4. THE BATTLE *TO* YOUR PROMISE..51

5. THE BATTLE *AT* YOUR PROMISE..65

6. THE BATTLE *IN* YOUR PROMISE..75

7. STAY IN YOUR PROMISE...85

8. STAY BATTLE READY...95

9. NEW LEVEL, NEW YOU...105

CONCLUSION..115

ABOUT THE AUTHOR..121

ADDITIONAL TITLES...123

INTRODUCTION

This book is not for everyone. Let's just establish that right now. This book is for those with faith.

The audacious people of God who are crazy enough to believe God just might want to use them to do something different and significant on this earth. The ones whom Jesus has been calling and training. The ones who have said, "Here I am, send me" in so many prayers they've lost count. Those who will do anything for the Lord.

Are you one of us? I believe you are.

There are a lot more of us than people think actually, although we don't always stand out in a crowd. We don't have a lot of stages to stand on to shout our message. We go to the grocery store like everyone else. We go out to grab coffee or go to the gym just like everyone else. Outwardly we look the same as those around us. *Inwardly, well, that's a different story.*

Within us beats a heart in sync with a different rhythm. Within us burns a fire. Within us is a passion to see Jesus be glorified and the Earth transformed into His image. Within us is the belief that it can happen…and it can happen through us!

My constant prayer is for these words to fan your flame into a wildfire of overflow, impact, and expansion. That you would find help for your journey with Jesus. That the Holy Spirit would bring clarity to your heart and direction for your next steps. It's not just a prayer, though. I truly know God will do this for you because He has done it for me time and again.

Editor's note to those who love grammar: For this book, we have chosen to differentiate between Israel's promised land, and your future promise land through past tense and present/future tense. The past tense "promised land" represents what Israel had been promised. The future tense "promise land" is what awaits you in your future.

CHAPTER ONE
THE EXPANSION MANDATE

1

The Expansion Mandate

We now begin the part of your journey when your insecurities finally fall by the wayside. There is a new you emerging. A you that is light, joyful, and carefree. Unburdened by the beliefs of yesterday. Unhindered by the previous pressures. Unplugged from the constant stream of negativity.

Your true identity has been unsealed, and it is already revealing itself. Do you see it? Do you want it? God is already calling it forth. God is inviting you into a journey of expansion and growth. Are you ready for it?

Don't just take my word for it, though. To me, the word "expansion" fits the understanding that we are moving from glory to glory in Christ. There is never a time when you are not moving from one place of glory to another.

As we do this we are navigating the ever-expanding kingdom of God that is all around us. My question to you is this: *"Do you know how to engage this ever-expanding kingdom of God?"*

This book is designed to bring insight into the in-between of those two glories. What happens when you go from one glory to the next? How does it happen? Why is it happening? That is what we are going to explore and hopefully shed some light on in the coming chapters.

I want to propose to you that you have been given the mandate to be fruitful, multiply, and expand. I am not suggesting that expansion looks a certain way, or is measured by a particular metric. The expanding life takes on many shapes and forms. While the "how" is up to God, the fact remains that we have been commanded by God to multiply our lives.

> "And God blessed them granting them certain authority and said to them, "Be fruitful, multiply, and fill the earth, and subjugate it putting it under your power; and rule over dominate the fish of the sea, the birds of the air, and every living thing that moves upon the earth." **Genesis 1:28 AMP**

Perhaps you only thought about this in reproductive terms? I know I did for a long time. The idea that God wanted to bless my life and increase me in many different ways was lost on me. When I read Genesis 1-3 it seemed to imply the multiplication command was about filling the Earth with children. While that is certainly the case, I believe it speaks to something more than only reproduction.

The concept of expansion, multiplication, and bearing fruit is literally throughout the entire Bible. Below I have listed some additional scriptures that imply either directly, or indirectly, that you are to multiply, to increase, and to expand. It is the way of the people of God.

Genesis 12:2-3 AMP

> "And I will make you a great nation, And I will bless you abundantly, And make your name great exalted, distin-

guished; And you shall be a blessing a source of great good to others; And I will bless, do good for, and benefit those who bless you. And I will curse that is, subject to My wrath and judgment, the one who curses despises, dishonors, has contempt for you. And in you all the families nations of the earth will be blessed."

Genesis 32:24-30 AMP

"So Jacob was left alone, and a Man came and wrestled with him until daybreak. When the Man saw that He had not prevailed against Jacob, He touched his hip joint; and Jacob's hip was dislocated as he wrestled with Him. Then He said, 'Let Me go, for day is breaking.' But Jacob said, 'I will not let You go unless You declare a blessing on me.' So He asked him, 'What is your name?' And he said, 'Jacob.'

And He said, 'Your name shall no longer be Jacob, but Israel; for you have struggled with God and with men and have prevailed.' Then Jacob asked Him, 'Please tell me Your name.' But He said, 'Why is it that you ask My name?' **And He declared a blessing of the covenant promises on Jacob there.** So, Jacob named the place Peniel the face of God, *saying*, 'For I have seen God face to face, yet my life has not been snatched away.'"

Deuteronomy 8:1-5 NIV

"Be careful to follow every command I am giving you today, so that you may live and increase and may enter and possess the land the Lord promised on oath to your ancestors. Remember how the Lord your God led you all the way in the wilderness these forty years, to humble and test you in order to know what was in your heart, whether or not you would keep his commands.

He humbled you, causing you to hunger and then feeding you with manna, which neither you nor your ancestors had known, to teach you that man does not live on bread alone but on every word that comes from the mouth of the Lord. Your clothes did not wear out and your feet did not swell during these forty years. Know then in your heart that as a man disciplines his son, so the Lord your God disciplines you."

Deuteronomy 1:11 AMP

"May the Lord, the God of your fathers, add to you a thousand times as many as you are and bless you, just as He has promised you!"

1 Chronicles 4:9-10 AMP

"Jabez was more honorable than his brothers; but his mother named him Jabez, saying, "Because I gave birth to him in pain." Jabez cried out to the God of Israel, saying, "Oh that You would indeed bless me and enlarge my border property, and that Your hand would be with me, and You would keep me from evil so that it does not hurt me!" And God granted his request."

Isaiah 54:2-3 NIV

"Enlarge the place of your tent, stretch your tent curtains wide, do not hold back; lengthen your cords, strengthen your stakes. For you will spread out to the right and to the left; your descendants will dispossess nations and settle their desolate cities."

Maybe you have read these passages promising blessing, increase, and expansion with a degree of separation. Maybe it feels like God was instructing *them* to do these things, but they don't necessarily apply to you. Maybe you have thought, *"I need Him to tell me directly before I will believe it."*

That was me. I hid behind a degree of separation from these words because I wanted a protective mechanism from being disappointed. It worked for a while until He did tell me directly.

When I was face to face with the rhema word of God I suddenly knew I could not hide anymore. I could not pass the buck to anyone else. I could not avoid it so I learned to embrace it; even if it meant facing my fear of it not happening.

As it is with all things God-related, embracing it was the most amazing thing! I feel frustrated that I ignored and denied this call to expansion for so long.

That protective mechanism, the one I felt I needed to avoid the pain of being let down? Yeah, it was hindering my walk with God. Why would I need protection from Him? How could I believe that He would have anything less than amazing things in store for me?

We do that, don't we? We hide from the good things of God. We listen to fear instead of faith. We trust experience over the word of God. We partner with invisibility because we fear what might happen if we shine too bright. We shrink ourselves in case these scriptures apply to other people, and not us.

Today you get to decide if you want to embrace this expansion mandate. Today you get to choose whether or not you can believe God for more of Him in your life. It will take courage. It will evoke obstacles. It will require faith. It will certainly be worth it.

The expansion mandate is the call to allow the God of abundance to reveal Himself through you.

THE EXPANSION MANDATE

It is the call to position yourself in a place of partnership with the Holy Spirit in a way that brings the kingdom of God powerfully into your life. It is a mandate of an overflowing life where the kingdom of God is alive *in* you, and moving *through* you onto the lives of those around you.

No one is exempt from this call. Not everyone will answer it, but no one is left out of it. You are called to **more.** You are invited to **more.** You are wanted in this **more.** You are needed in the **more.**

More faith is available. More peace is attainable. More joy is accessible. More love, more self-control, more resources, more confidence and so much more are included in this mandate. More is just a word to describe the work of Jesus in our life.

Paul was shedding light on this when he wrote 2 Corinthians 3:18-19. Read it for yourself in your favorite translation. I've provided the Amplified Bible Translation, my favorite, below.

> "And we all, with unveiled face, continually seeing as in a mirror the glory of the Lord, **are progressively being transformed into His image from one degree of glory to even more glory,** which comes from the Lord, who is the Spirit." **2 Corinthians 3:18-19 AMP**

This is the work of God in your life. It is always happening around you, whether you want it to or not. You are being made into a greater likeness of Christ. You are being continually perfected. You are going from your place with the Lord right now (your current measure of glory) to an even greater place.

This is what the Holy Spirit does for everyone in Christ Jesus. He is always leading, shaping, and upgrading your life.

A popular, and powerful prophecy illustrates this aspect of God's heart so well. We cannot explore expansion without including the famous scripture in Isaiah 54:1-3 that many have received as a prophetic word. My husband and I have received this prophetic word so many times. Each time we have received it we have been ushered into a new season of growth, change, and expansion.

In my study of these verses, I have found some powerful truths that help illustrate the heart of God for your expansion. There are a few cultural and historical factors I want to share with you that help modern-day readers understand the deeper meaning of this passage. Read it below before we unpack it.

> **"Sing, oh barren woman,** you who never bore a child; burst into song, shout for joy, you who were never in labor; because more are the children of the desolate woman than of her who has a husband," says the Lord.
>
> **"Enlarge the place of your tent**, stretch your tent curtains wide, do not hold back; lengthen your cords, strengthen your stakes. **For you will spread out to the right and to the left;** your descendants will dispossess nations and settle in their desolate cities." **Isaiah 54:1-3 NIV**

When we read these Old Testament prophecies we need to ask ourselves a few questions to unlock the application for our lives.

1. When was this prophecy given? This helps us know if it has already been fulfilled. It also helps us put the words in the context of Jesus' death and resurrection. The cross compels us to look at prophecies of judgment through a lens of grace.

2. Who was this prophecy given to? What was their culture like? This provides greater context for the imagery in the words.

3. What was the purpose of the word? What was God trying to accomplish in the people through this instruction or warning?

When examining the Isaiah 54 prophecy through these three questions we reveal some fascinating insights. This prophecy was given to Israel while she was in Babylonian captivity around 538 BC, hundreds of years after Israel arrived in her promised land.

THE EXPANSION MANDATE

This word of hope was given to the people of God who were living in captivity and humiliation, after having been removed from the promised land.

In ancient biblical times, people often lived in tents, as Abraham did. This style of living went on for generations, but at the time Isaiah's prophecy was given the vast majority of Israelites did not live in tents. They lived in more permanent homes.

Why would God prophecy about expanding tents when the people no longer lived in tents? I believe it was an intentional decision to point the Israelites' focus to a time filled with promises that had already been fulfilled.

Using the language of tent expansion was an invitation to remember the faithfulness of God.

It was a reminder of the way He met their forefathers, and how He did what he said He would do. Here again, God is telling His people to expect great things. He is telling them to expect an increase and expansion. He is telling them to prepare for it now.

In the same breath, He is reminding them that He does what He says. That their faith is worth risking because His track record is trustworthy. He wrapped this word that was undoubtedly uncomfortable to receive in the comfort of His proven faithfulness.

His kindness to His people was displayed in the hope of the goodness this expansion would bring, the comfort His faithfulness evokes, and the awareness of their current circumstances.

Isaiah 54:1-3 was addressed to the women because **it was historically the women's job to tend to the tents.** They made them, fixed them, and moved to them. When they would pick up and move to a different area for fresh water and resources it was the women who would pack up the tents. When they arrived in the new land the women would set the tents up again.

The tent material was a fabric made of goat hair clippings that the women would weave together tightly. Yes, goat hair! It would take them about a year to collect enough goat hair to weave a new patch of the tent when a section was wearing out.

As you can imagine, expanding a tent was not a quick and easy task. They did not simply stretch the hide to make more room. The tent was not animal leather at all. When new additions came into the family through marriage or child birth the tent would be expanded to make room. This process would take a year at minimum for an average family.

The imagery of God telling the women to start preparing for bigger tents is the imagery of a woman today building another 2000 square feet onto her home before she is even pregnant with her first child. To invest the time and resources into that endeavor you must be convinced that many children are in your future.

This was, and is, God's invitation to His people. Do the work of expansion because expansion is coming. Do the preparation work because it will take a lot of time, and expansion is coming. Get ready because when you need the space you will not have the time or energy to make the space.

The concept of preparation is largely lost on us. Nearly everything we want can be done quickly or can be bought from someone who has already done the preparation. **As a result, our culture has lost touch with the time needed to truly prepare.**

I used to read this prophecy through my modern American eyes. I envisioned that you could just pull the tent fabric hard and stretch it out to make the room needed. It seemed like an invitation to use brute force to expand rather than time and patience.

While civilization may have advanced the ways of God are still unchanged. God is not obligated to speed up His process simply because we are not used to the amount of time it takes to grow hair out. Good things take time, preparation, and patience.

Notice that Isaiah prophecies, "Do not hold back" in verse two. This prophetic word was a command.

THE EXPANSION MANDATE

The size of our preparation will determine the size of the increase.

Just as Jesus preached in the parable of the talents, how we steward the instruction greatly affects the result.

A large tent needs a strong infrastructure under it. These tents had multiple rooms separated by goat hair curtains for privacy. There were apartments for the men to gather, rooms for the women to sleep with their children, and other rooms depending on the size and wealth of the family.

For example, Jacob's wealth allowed him to have completely separate tents of many rooms for his wives, something that would have been very rare at that time.

I love how detailed God is. I love that He included a note about the cords and tent pegs. I just imagine Him telling Isaiah, *"This is going to be HUGE. We are going to need new tent pegs! Stronger tent cords. This is going to be wonderful!"*

His emphasis on the infrastructure of the tent helps us understand how excellent God is. A large tent fabric is worthless if there is not an infrastructure strong enough to hold it up.

How strong is your infrastructure? Could you support the weight of a large tent-sized increase mentally, physically, or spiritually? God intends to make you strong. He does this by stretching you and building internal strength within you.

He is already preparing you for expansion. It is time to realize that the things He has you doing right now are the goat clippings of tomorrow's new tent piece.

Some of us have already heard His call to expand us. We know expansion and increase are coming, and we are doing our best to partner with that process.

Others of us are looking at the bag of goat hair in our hand wondering how on Earth this can become anything other than garbage.

THE EXPANSION MANDATE

How will God make a big, fancy tent out of *this*?

It is a challenge to stay connected to faith and belief in the bigger promise when we are watching goat hair grow. The monotony of growth causes many of us to give up the belief that something great could come from these small, repetitive motions.

If the ho hum of monotony is draining you it is probably because you are not yet completely convinced you need a bigger tent. This is faith's moment to shine. If you truly believed God was bringing increase to you, would you operate differently? I suspect you would not meagerly clip the hair only when it is convenient.

If you really believed this mandate, you would feed those goats vitamins so their hair grows faster. You would do what you could to get more goats to increase the amount of hair you had available.

If you are struggling to imagine what your life would look like with God's expansion you are not alone. Most of us don't dare to hope for this kind of prophecy because it is far too risky to dream of it. I want to be clear; this word was not given to people living in abundance and greatness.

The Israelites were not in a position to shine when they received this prophecy. No one expected anything good to come from them. The ode to the barren women in verse 1 was the connecting point God was making to their current state.

The Israelites were in captivity when they received this word. They were shamed, disgraced, and exiled far from home. Nothing felt familiar. Nothing was working for them. Nothing was easy. They were metaphorically barren with no hope, and nothing to show for their lives.

If I can take the liberty of paraphrasing this into our modern context, I think it would sound something like this:

I see where you are right now. I see how increase and expansion feels like an impossibility. But I am coming to do great things through you. I am coming to advance and increase you. Prepare for it because you know me to be a God of my word. Spare no expense as you prepare. Do not hold back wondering how much I will expand you. Go all the way, do all the things because I am coming to do everything I said I would do.

When we allow ourselves to partner with the expansion mandate the monotony in our life is exchanged with vision.

What has felt meaningless begins to be filled with purpose because we understand what is at stake. We allow ourselves to look forward to it, which is the beginning work of faith.

Expansion is coming to the body of Christ. The increase is already here and multiplying in our midst. He has said it and He is doing it. We are all invited to be a part of this if we are willing to do the work of partnering with the Holy Spirit.

How do we partner with this expansion? I am not suggesting you go out and buy a few goats and shears. I am, however, suggesting you take an honest look at your life. Ask the Holy Spirit to highlight the thoughts and beliefs that are hindering you. Invite His work into your life in a greater measure.

There is a pattern to how the Lord works in our lives. There is a rhythm He follows. The steps may vary from person to person, but the pattern remains the same. This pattern is like the process of building muscle.

I'm no athlete, but I do know some things about human biology. I know that building muscle first requires breaking it down. We put stress and weight on it, allow it to break down a bit, and then it heals stronger. The more we repeat this pattern the more the muscle grows big and strong.

This is what spiritual growth is like. There is a process and it is fairly predictable from one season to the next. Sure, the circumstances change, but the rhythm beats on. On our expansion journey, we will be met with a series of challenges I am going to call battles.

These are spiritual battles we will find ourselves in at different stages of our growth that cannot be avoided.

However, the length of the battle, and the recovery time after our victory can be shortened as we begin to understand how these battles can serve our expansion.

The four battles we win on the journey to expansion are:

1. The battle *for* the promise
2. The battle *to* the promise
3. The battle *at* the promise
4. The battle *in* the promise

Every one of us moves through this pattern as God advances, increases, multiplies, and expands our lives. Before we dive into those four battles, we need to look at another essential example of the expansion mandate.

In the next chapter, we will examine the pattern of expansion God brought into the lives of several biblical figures and the implications that has on our lives.

CHAPTER TWO
BLESSED! A THOUSANDS TIMES, BLESSED!

2

Blessed, A Thousand Times, Blessed!

God is a God of blessing. God has chosen to make us in His image. Because of this, we are truly blessed! The goal of this chapter is to show you how deeply the evidence of the abundant, overflowing, increasing blessing of God is well established throughout the Bible.

Yet despite what I would consider to be concrete "proof" of this truth, the people of God continue to struggle with it. The idea that God wants to deeply bless us is so hard for many of us to believe, but this characteristic of God's nature is not reserved for Him alone.

It is part of who He is, and it is part of what He has invited us into as well. We are to reflect Him, and if we want to do this accurately, we must become comfortable with the idea that God will bless us to make Himself known through the visibility of that blessing.

A Jewish scholar once said that God's favorite form of evangelism was through jealousy. As uncomfortable as I felt the first time I heard those words, they have remained to me the most accurate way to explain what we see in the Bible.

In the Old Testament, we consistently find stories of God blessing His people and only His people. Stories where the blessing of God was so thick it caused problems for other people groups.

In the New Testament, we find Jesus becoming that blessing. He speaks of that hope of blessing amid cultural and natural hardships. We find the people of God feeling empowered, blessed, and full of hope despite everyone else's attempt to stifle the joy within them. That counter-cultural difference led many to come to know Jesus and still does to this day.

We may not be comfortable with this "method," but God certainly is. He will increase any of us who are willing to allow Him to. He will bless every one of us who ask, often to the point of the conversion of others. He truly is that good!

I hope you are reading this at a moment in time when you already know this. Likely you have already known of His overflowing blessing that comes in all shapes in forms. If that is the case, I encourage you to read the pages of this chapter with an open heart to go deeper.

Ask the Holy Spirit to show you again the wonderful power of His blessing at work in your life.

If you are new to this concept, I only ask you to read with an open mind. I am not presenting anything based on opinion or experience alone, but Biblical facts. I would ask you to take a moment to consider this question:

Who benefits from your refusal to partner with God's blessing?

I know. Those are strong words. I wrote them from my heart because that was me. I felt so selfish praying for blessing. I felt downright guilty about it. It was such a bad idea to me that I regularly judged my brothers and sisters in Christ who embraced God's blessing in a way I couldn't bring myself to.

At my core, I didn't believe God loved me enough to entrust anything to me. On other days, I was so convinced I would screw it up that I didn't even try. Oh to know then what I know now!

A pastor I respect articulates this so well. He says that in the core of those who only feel comfortable asking God for the bare minimum, we find a selfish heart. This may be a surprising thought. He goes on to say that only saying prayers for our own needs is the most selfish form of prayer one could pray.

To only ask for our own needs is to say that the other people around us don't matter to us, or that we don't see their needs. Even worse, we somehow don't believe God could use us to help meet their needs.

However, we, as believers, are the answer to the problems around us. We hold the keys to Heaven through Jesus. Why would we use that connection only to solve our own problems?

This is true on a spiritual, emotional, physical, and financial level. Your ability to walk in peace, have joy in abundance, and be filled with hope is an answer to the problems around you. It is also part of the blessing of God.

God wants to bless you!

Our worldview as sons and daughters of God is different. We know where we are going when we die. We know how the story of the world ends, and we know it's great news for everyone in Christ. This should awaken a hunger for more blessings within us.

Let's look at some pivotal moments in Biblical history where God's desire to bless became the central focus.

Starting in Genesis 2, we draw our attention to the garden God created for mankind. This was not a small backyard with a few sun-scorched hydrangeas and a half-dead fern. This was an expansive place dripping with all kinds of blessings. Part of the garden even held gold.

My Bible makes a point to note it was "good gold!" There were gemstones like onyx. Some trees were pleasing to the eye and good for food. This is a picture of a great place. Nothing seems to have been spared in this garden. Right from the start the message was clear. Everything God does is excellent.

Genesis 12 draws our attention to God's desire to make a people for Himself. He calls Abram into a nomadic journey to become the people of God. He blesses Abram. **He really blesses Him.**

Abram becomes Abraham and begins to grow in all kinds of ways. He grows wealthy and adds more servants, animals, and bigger tents as a result of this. What happened? God blessed him.

I think it is important to note that God's blessing did not eliminate all the problems in Abraham's life. Far from it, actually. But the blessing was there because God put it there. God is a God of blessing, increase, and expansion. What we choose to do with that is up to us.

Through the stories of Abraham, Isaac, Jacob, and Joseph we see the story of blessing repeating itself. The blessing of God was (and is) very powerful. It was life-altering for all who received it. When they received the blessing their life began to increase and expand in the most unexpected ways.

Through Joseph's story, we finally get to see how instrumental this blessing can become for the lives of those around us. Joseph was different. He treated his blessing differently. He seemed to embrace it more fully than his father and grandfathers did.

What was the result? He partnered with God to save countless people from dying of starvation, including his own family. You can read the story for yourself in Genesis 37-46.

From this point on, the multiplication effect of God's blessing becomes more and more clear. One man or woman connected to God's heart received vital help, and the people around him/her were truly blessed. Their world began to expand under the blessing, and lives were changed forever.

Exodus 2 calls our attention to Jochebed, the wife of a Levite in slavery in Egypt. This woman discerned there was something different about her baby. Could we assume they blessed this baby? It seems to be the case.

God's blessing was on this baby because, when she put him in a basket and sent him down the river hoping for a miracle, the miracle came.

Pharaoh's daughter found the baby, thus saving him from the fate of all other Hebrew boys at that time. Meant for the slaughter, God blessed this child named Moses, and that blessing stayed with him throughout his life.

You likely know the story of Moses, the man who liberated the Hebrews from four hundred years of slavery and delivered them to the border of the promised land. This blessing not only saved his life, but it expanded his life.

It opened doors that had not been opened for any other child in that generation. It positioned him to increase in such a way he became one of the greatest prophets, eventually speaking with God face to face.

Three hundred years later another young man received a similar blessing that liberated, delivered, and changed the course of the people of God again. David, the outcast shepherd boy, received this blessing.

Samuel, the prophet, anointed him as the next king of Israel in a private ceremony. God sent Samuel to the middle of nowhere to bless a nobody, and that blessing carried tremendous power.

You know the story of this nobody who goes on to understand something of the blessing few before him, or since, understood. God blesses on behalf of His people for His glory. The blessing didn't come because these people were inherently special. It certainly didn't come because of their good works, or exceptional moral fortitude.

God puts it on whoever He can for the sake of the people. Yes, the individual increases. Yes, they get favor, and often wealth because of it. But the sentiment of Abraham's blessing remains the central theme...blessed *to be* a blessing.

The blessing is not an end in itself; it is a beginning. It is a positioning and aligning under the reality of God. David is the perfect example of what the blessing was for. Well, the first part of his story demonstrates this better than the latter half.

Perhaps David's downfall and Moses's mistake are reasons why we shy away from this powerful blessing of God.

It is sobering to see how badly a good story can end. But can we honestly point to these downfalls as a result of God blessing them? Of course not! We are no more destined to screw up than they were. Character matters. Humility matters. Our regular pursuit of God's heart helps us steward His blessing without going astray.

For Moses, it was his unchecked anger that got the best of him. Yet despite being barred from the promised land, **God's mercy still allowed him to see it with his physical eyes.**

For David, God's mercy allowed his family line, as twisted and distorted as it was, to eventually become the physical protection of God Himself. Joseph, the descendant of David, protected Mary as she brought forth Jesus. God regularly spoke to Joseph about coming threats to baby Jesus, and David's legacy got to be greatly redeemed in the end.

What would your life look like if this kind of Biblical blessing came and rested on you?

What things would change? What issues would you want to address so they didn't hinder you? What relationships would you let go of? What kinds of projects would you want to get involved with if you knew this kind of blessing was resting on you?

With the arrival of Jesus, the blessing of God begins to take a new, fresh shape. No longer was the blessing for one or two key people

on behalf of the whole nation. Through the resurrection, and the baptism of the Holy Spirit, this same blessing became available to everyone.

I cannot even believe I get to write these words! All these years later this truth is still so mind-blowing to me. God, you are amazing! **Jesus opened a door of blessing for us that few take advantage of.** I am not talking about salvation, although He obviously opened that door.

To me, salvation is the entry point to the house. If we stop on that front threshold we will miss so much of what Jesus has given to us. The real blessing is in the proverbial house of His blessing. Now the blessing is HIM!

Let's take this a step further. What is more powerful: the blessing or **the one who blesses?**

The one who blesses, right? The one who can bestow this powerful blessing we have just been reading about must be more powerful than the blessing itself because He was able to give it. That means He has more than that to give. This should give us great hope and joy! The Blesser is not just for you, not just in love with you, but within you!

This same blessing that brought forth an entire tribe of people from a barren couple **is within you.** This same blessing that preserved Joseph through so much hardship, while increasing and expanding his life, so he could save an entire nation from famine **is within you.**

This same blessing that opened doors for Moses to liberate millions of people from four hundred years of slavery, supernaturally providing for them and protecting them **is within you.**

This same blessing that anointed David and ushered Israel into a new era of freedom **is within you.** This same blessing that raised Christ from the dead **is within you!**

We are barely scratching the surface of the work of God's blessing with these stories. What I want to know is why would anyone reject this? Why would anyone hide from the Blesser Himself?

You have been blessed. Not only that, but you have been blessed so you can become a blessing to those around you.

This book is all about expansion.

More importantly, it is about *how* to receive this blessing to expand your life in Christ. To increase and expand you have to settle that you have been blessed. There cannot be any more wondering and there cannot be any doubt. You, yes you, have received this same blessing as your forefathers and mothers.

You have received the kind of blessing that is life-altering. It is eternity-shaking. It is mind-blowing. The reality of your blessing is not up for debate for those who are in Christ Jesus. The real question is how are you partnering with it? Are you in denial? Are you ignoring it? Are you wrestling with it? Or are you embracing it?

Take a moment to read Deuteronomy 1:11 and let Moses' prayer sink into your heart. Read these words as though they are God's prayer for you because they are!

> "May the Lord, the God of your Ancestors, increase you a thousand times, and bless you as He has promised!"
> **Deuteronomy 1:11 NIV**

You have been blessed. You may not feel like it. Your life may not be reflecting it, but it is true. You have been and are being blessed. Full stop. End of story. So, what happens now? You own it.

Get clear on the way this blessing moves through your unique calling. Strap on your armor and get ready for the battle *for* the promise.

CHAPTER THREE
THE BATTLE *FOR* THE PROMISE

3

The Battle *FOR* The Promise

God is a God of promises. He loves to make them and He loves to keep them. He loves promises so much there are at least **7,487 promises to people recorded in the Bible.** It took Everett R. Storms, a school teacher from Canada, eighteen months to find them all.

In fact, Everett read the Bible more than twenty-seven times to find as many as 8,810 recorded promises. And yet, the English word "promise" does not exist in Biblical Hebrew.

These thousands of words were not promises as we understand promises today. A lot of us hear the word "promise" and tend to think of it as a loose commitment. We don't live in a handshake society anymore, and we can be suspicious of someone who wants us to take them at their word.

Let's be honest, promises are broken all the time, even by people we love dearly. Because of this, most of us don't pay much attention when someone says they promise to do something. Personally, I find that most people "promise" as a form of manipulation, whether they intend to or not.

Your kid "promises" to keep their room clean if you give them ice cream, but two days later it's messy yet again. Your boss promises a promotion if you work harder, and then gives it to someone else. Your parent promises to take you shopping if you get good grades, but doesn't makes the time.

We know that promises can be broken with little to no consequence or legal action. Yes, that promise-breaker's reputation could take a hit, but other than that? We have become good at just letting it go. To most of us, a promise just doesn't mean much.

When we apply this perspective to the promises we find in the Bible we miss what God is saying entirely. **The English definition of the word "promise" is not in the Bible.**

These 7,487 promises were not good intentions. They were not great ideas that turned out to be too hard to execute. They were not merely words from a smooth-talker who had no intention of following through.

The promises in the Bible were vows.

They were what we would consider to be legal contracts with actionable consequences if results were not delivered. In the Old Testament, God used words like "speak," "say," and "word," instead of promise. God's promises were His intentions. They were His obligations that He imposed on Himself. **They were facts describing a future reality He could already see.**

My favorite example of this is the ceremony God had with Abraham in Genesis 15. God had just promised Abraham land, children, and more. The story goes on to describe a covenant ceremony that was a common custom of the time.

Ancient historical documents from the Middle East detail a ceremony that two parties would perform when entering a covenant agreement together.

THE BATTLE FOR THE PROMISE

After the parties had agreed on the terms they would select several animals. They would kill them, split them in two, and position them in a way that would allow all the blood to pool down in a little stream. All parties involved in the covenant would walk through the blood purposely getting it on them.

The ceremony was an agreement of what would happen if one party broke the terms of the covenant. Essentially, after this ceremony, you had the right to cut that person open if they did not do as they had promised.

God had Abraham get everything ready. Per the custom, both God and Abraham were to pass through the blood to ratify the covenant; but then something most unexpected happened.

God put Abraham to sleep and a smoking firepot moved through the blood on behalf of God. He did not allow Abraham to participate in the ceremony. **By doing this, God took all the responsibility of keeping this covenant onto Himself.**

Abraham was now free to stray from the terms, but God was not. **This is such a powerful picture of true Biblical promise.** When God invites us into His promise He takes on the obligation of the fulfillment. Our job is to stay close to Him, allow Him to grow us, and do what He says. He takes care of the rest.

God has made vows to you.

He has contractually obligated Himself to you in the most glorious way. He saw the future you, and committed Himself to helping you become that person, taking on all the cost of your transformation. Your promise land is guaranteed and insured through Him.

Through scripture, God has vowed that you will have victory over your four battles on the way to your promise land. It is promised in the most assured way possible. While He takes on the bulk of the expense there are a few things we can do to make this journey easier.

After all, the journey to your promise land is not a leisurely stroll down the beach with a gentle breeze moving through your hair. It is much more like a Jumanji game of treacherous adventure with the incredible presence of God all around you. Sounds exciting, doesn't it?

These four battles cannot be avoided.

You will need to fight them if you want to enter your promise. As unavoidable as they are, there are some things you can do to avoid delay, backtracking, and prolonging the journey. This is my heart with writing this book. I want to do whatever I can to help you avoid all the unnecessary stops because this process is long enough without it.

I need to pause for a moment and ask for a little creative liberty. To illustrate the process of these four battles we are going to look at the life of Israel from their deliverance in Exodus through their battle at Jericho as though Israel was one person.

If you know this story you know that Israel's journey through these moments took well over forty years, and involved multiple generations of people. For our purposes, we will treat Israel as if she was one person going through all four of these battles because you and I follow this same pattern in our own lives.

Our first battlefield appears in Egypt where Israel is not herself. She has been beaten down, seemingly abandoned by her God, and living in slavery for the past four hundred years.

That means that at least three generations were born into, and lived entirely enslaved, with no knowledge of any other way of life. She was suffering. She was hopeless. She had completely forgotten that she was God's beloved bride.

Israel could not dream of a promise. There was no point in dreaming at all. There was no "home" for her outside of Egypt. Her former home had been re-settled by other people. She didn't know where she belonged. Can you relate to this?

At the beginning of all of our promise journeys, we come to learn there is more for us. That more, however, will come at great cost. We often feel called out and away from what has been. We can't always explain it, but we know the winds of change have been blowing, calling us forward.

To pursue another vision will require change. It will require courage. It will require the ability to dream beyond this current reality into something that might be better, but we aren't fully convinced.

The grass could be greener over there, or there could be no grass at all. Even a familiar hell can feel better than an unfamiliar heaven, and this is why many of us stall out before the journey even begins.

To get to your promise land you have to believe there is one out there for you.

You have to trust that God has good things in store for you. You have to believe it is God calling out to you from your future promise, and not some phantom voice that wants to enslave you even more.

I am not going to define your promise land for you because I don't know what God is calling you to do. I only know that He is calling you to something more. He is inviting you to expand and increase. And if He hasn't called you yet, He will soon.

Your promise land is as unique to you as your fingerprint. It is the meeting place of your calling, your assignment, your breakthroughs, and your legacy. Only God knows the boundary lines around it.

I am on my sixth promise land journey because the boundary lines of our promise are always expanding. At first, my promise was a Godly family, and He got me there. Then it was the call to ministry, and He expanded me into that.

Our promise land expanded again with an out-of-state move, then a career change, and so on. As we will see from Israel's journey, the promised land often begins as a final destination, but soon becomes much more than that.

The battle *for* your promise is the battle to receive more of God's vision for your life.

God knows you won't move forward until you know where you are going. He knows you want to see where you are going before you commit to uprooting your life.

He also knows the complete vision of you that He sees would be far too overwhelming for you to ingest. So He gives us bite-size pieces that are tantalizing enough to move us to action, but not so overwhelming that we count ourselves out before we even get started.

Israel's first battle displays this well. We enter her story with Moses showing up in Egypt with a vision from God. He received that first bite and it was amazing.

He is so compelled by His encounter with God that he makes his way back to Egypt, something he never thought he would do again. With Aaron by his side, he draws on the memory of the burning bush to summon the courage required to accomplish this call.

Moses gathers the elders of the Israelites and shares his encounter. He announces that God wants more for Israel's life, and just like that, the first battle cry is sounded.

The announcement of the call to something more is the invitation to the battlefield. From this point forward we will face all kinds of adversity. We are being set up to witness a display of God's power on our behalf.

We read this story in Exodus 4:31. The response of the elders as Moses told them the amazing things God said about them was so moving. Their first response was to believe!

> "**and they believed.** And when they heard that the Lord was concerned about them and had seen their misery, they bowed down and worshiped." **Exodus 4:31 NIV**

Isn't that beautiful? God saw Israel's misery, and He sees yours. If this is the battle you find yourself in take comfort that He sees you, and He has come to bring you out!

The battle *for* the promise is our battle for stepping into our identity as a son or daughter of God. It is the realignment of our vision of ourselves and His vision of us.

Before we can get to the promise we must realize there is a promise. We have to receive that promise, and this is what this first battle is all about.

Exodus 4:31 is so beautiful to me because it is the authentic, pure response to great news. If only the story moved from this precious moment to the Israelites packing up their things, walking straight up to their new land, opening a welcome basket, and living happily ever after! We all know that is not what happened.

Israel had this wonderful moment of pure worship, and then she found out that Pharaoh was doubling her workload. She realized this would not be an easy victory, and she began to hate the word of deliverance.

She began to blame the word of hope instead of trusting in it. She struggled to understand what God was doing. She was on an emotional rollercoaster!

Israel did not get free from Egypt because she greatly believed in God's promise. It was not her faith that opened the door, it was God's faithfulness. But Israel did get one thing right. **When the door to leave was opened (through the final plague) she got up and walked out.**

What would have happened if Israel had stayed? What if she thought God's promise was not a vow but a fun idea with no guarantee? What if they stayed in their houses and hid in fear that God's faithfulness had run out after all those plagues and wonders?

Pharaoh was ready to kill them all at the Red Sea. We can assume they would have been killed in their homes, or forced into worse conditions for hundreds of years to come.

Your battle *for* your promise will require your cooperation, but God knows you cannot do it on your own. He will open the doors for you. **You just need to be ready to go when He clears the roadblocks for you.** The battle *for* our promise does not need to take long.

This battle will last as long as it takes you to believe.

On this battlefield, God is repositioning you so you can see yourself more accurately according to how He sees you. He is making a way for you to hear from Him, and receive what He wants to say. He is preparing your heart to receive the promise He intends to bring you into.

I remember times in this battle when I would say to the Lord, *"Why do I have to change? I am doing what you told me to do?"* The Israelites could have easily said this as well.

After all, it was God that brought them to Egypt all those years ago. The truth is, you don't have to change. You can stay right where you are. **But, if you choose to stay, you will miss the greater glory of His expanding promise.**

God will simply wait for you right there until you are ready. He is not going to change His plan because you are not ready to follow Him. He is more patient than we could ever imagine and He will gladly wait for us to get on board with His plan. Our refusal to follow becomes our first opportunity to partner with delay.

None of us want to intentionally delay God's plan for our life. When your spouse asks you, "What's your plan for the day?" None of us respond with, "I am planning to delay God's promise and make it harder for Him to work with me."

We don't want to delay, but we do. Israel did as well. In some ways, we could rename Israel's journey to her promised land as "the dance of delay." Israel was masterful at the art of delay, and if I am being fully transparent, I've been there too.

Let's look at a few things that can cause delays in our journey:

- Ignoring God's call
- Assuming you are not capable of doing what He said, and therefore rejecting it
- Refusing to see the good to come
- Seeing yourself as God's victim thinking He always makes you do the hard stuff
- Complaining
- Not obeying His word and/or instruction
- Negativity

There are more ways to partner with delay but negativity just might be one of the most dangerous. God does not like negativity, and I don't like that. I don't like the way people have made me feel like I can't be honest with God, because sometimes that honesty involves negative feelings. This is not the kind of negativity God dislikes.

True negativity is essentially believing and speaking out the plans of the enemy. True negativity lacks hope. It is void of vision. It cannot trust God, and that is why God doesn't like it. Negativity will have you hiding in the house when God has opened the door to freedom for you.

Negativity is the fruit of cynicism, and cynicism is the fruit of hopelessness. When we trace it to the root we are negative because we don't believe God. Hopelessness is simply not having any hope. Since we have been given so many reasons to hope in God hopelessness is actually disobedience. Can you see why God doesn't like negativity?

As you prepare to move out of this battle you need to leave negativity behind.

This doesn't mean you can't have bad days, can't feel angry about life, or that you have to pretend all the time. It means that you challenge every single speck of hopelessness within you. Take it captive **and replace it with the vows God has made you** in His word. When you address the hopelessness you will find you are less and less negative.

The hard truth is there are no pessimists in Heaven. Once a pessimist gets to heaven, they are immediately transformed into an optimist; because it is impossible to be without God's goodness at the center of everything there.

If it is true in Heaven, it can be true on Earth. You don't need negativity. It is not helping you become more like Jesus, and it just might be delaying you from receiving the promise you have been praying for.

You will eventually leave this battlefield with so much excitement surrounding the dream of this new promise. **To me, there is not much more exhilarating than feeling truly called and promised something by God.**

If only we left these moments and immediately stepped into our promise land. In truth, we step forward with a spring in our step right into the longest stretch of the journey as we make our way *to* our promise.

CHAPTER FOUR
THE BATTLE *TO* THE PROMISE

4

The Battle *TO* the promise

With Israel's first battle behind her and the promised land in front of her, **she made her way into the great unknown. Expansion was already breaking forth.** The air was lighter with her enemy dead at the bottom of the Red Sea.

Her body was enjoying peace, and the memories of hard labor were beginning to fade. Her children had space to run. Life seemed hopeful as she looked ahead.

How quickly that good feeling evaporated in that desert! Within a matter of days, she was cranky, thirsty, and filled with regret. She began to wonder, *"How could my new freedom be this bad?"* That is something I, myself, have wondered on more than one occasion.

Life after the first battle is disorienting. It is unfamiliar and it is puzzling. We can be simultaneously longing for what used to be while hoping for what is to come; which is very draining. What used to bring comfort often doesn't anymore, and we hardly recognize ourselves.

Some would call this "transition" and they would be right. God has brought you "out" but He has not yet brought you "in."

Knowing the future promise feels good, in some ways, but now we find ourselves on the long road to the fulfillment of that promise. Everything is changing. Our provision changes. Our daily schedule changes. Our relationships change. We are new, but we don't feel new. We feel a little lost...and we are.

Perhaps this battle is the longest of the four battles for a reason. Something is happening behind the scenes of our lives that is radical, specific, and necessary.

> **In the journey *to* the promise,
> we become who we really are.**

The part of us that only God sees. The person who is capable of the thing God has promised. The person who will steward that promise well and not squander it. Because we are not just journeying *to* the promise, we are becoming carriers *of* His promise.

Promise carriers are a different breed of people. We are unstoppable and unwavering in our understanding of who God is. We have come to see the world as He sees it, carrying His vision to the best of our abilities. We are comfortable in the presence of God because it has become home to us. We look forward to being used by the Lord to bring His kingdom to the Earth.

Becoming a promise carrier does not happen overnight. It is a long process where the onion of our heart is peeled back and transformed one layer at a time. The wilderness works to expose us so God can heal us. It helps us discover where we need an upgrade in our thinking. **The rivers of the wilderness wash our wounds and purify our hearts.**

This is what the battle *to* the promise is supposed to be, but it is often the place where we lose our way. Far too many people lay down and die on this battlefield. They misread the moment. They tap out. They make their bed in the wilderness, having become so disoriented and disillusioned, they just can't go any further in their faith.

This battle becomes the end of their expansion journey. They have chosen to settle for a life of wandering in limitation because they have stopped believing there is a place flowing with milk and honey awaiting them.

As challenging as this leg of the journey is, there are ways to avoid making it worse. When Israel came out of her battle *for* the promise she failed pretty badly, and her second battle lasted way longer than it was supposed to. Thankfully her story provides us with insights into pitfalls we can avoid on our journey.

Let's pick up her story in Exodus 14. Israel has just experienced the deliverance of a lifetime as she walked across dry ground in the Red Sea. You have to read it for yourself because it is an incredible story! After every single Israelite foot was safely across the sea Moses lifted his hands, and the water came rushing in, drowning all of the Egyptian enemies.

> **She entered the desert, and unbeknownst to her, stepped onto her second battlefield.**

Her promised land was only about an eleven-day walking journey from Egypt. Yes, it was a difficult journey, but she was free! That should be enough to quiet the questions rising in her, right?

Even though she had very little water or food, God supernaturally provided for her every time she asked. Despite His miraculous generosity, Israel complained. Actually, she couldn't stop complaining.

She forgot to leave her negativity and pessimism in Egypt, and it was costly. But that was not the only thing that cost her. As I mentioned in the previous chapter, Israel became a master at delay, and this desert is where she perfected her craft.

But God had a job to do on this journey *to* the promised land, and that job was to transform Israel into His likeness.

She needed to be like Him to represent Him to the other people groups. All those years in bondage had done a number on her. God was adamant to prove His faithfulness and character to her so she would learn to trust Him again.

For example, when Israel was thirsty He provided water through supernatural means. First, it was a log thrown into a bitter river that made the water drinkable. Then He provided water flowing out of a rock. When she was hungry He provided manna for her to eat.

His provision was miraculous but she had to actively participate in the miracle. She had to daily collect this miracle food. Why did He do that? It was part of her preparation.

He was teaching her character development, integrity, the principles of His provision, and more. When they quickly grew tired of eating only manna God provided enormous amounts of quail for them to eat. **Every single miracle God worked on Israel's behalf was intentional.** God can do anything, so when He does something specific it is significant.

This second battle is about getting to know God on a deeper level, getting to know ourselves, and learning the details of the new way of life He is bringing us into. We battle to trust Him. We fight to believe He is telling us the truth. We fight to develop Godly character traits within ourselves.

The battle *to* our promise is the place we fight for our connection with Him.

The promise God has brought you *to* is a shared vision. It is as much about Him as it is about you. He cannot bring you into it until you are ready to be there with Him in deep communion.

Israel seemed to struggle with this. I am sure the generations of exposure to pagan gods had rubbed off on her. She was not comfortable being close to God. She certainly didn't trust him, either.

There were a couple of big mistakes in her first days in the desert. These choices revealed just how much she would need to grow and change before she could carry her promise and the blessing that would come with it.

First, it took her three full days to even ask God for water in that desert. That means she was close to dying of thirst before she had the guts to approach this same God who had just miraculously delivered her!

Second, she rejected the presence of God time and again. She seemed to be more interested in ritualistic distance than the close connection God wanted.

> "And the Lord said to Moses, 'Go to the people and consecrate them today and tomorrow. Have them wash their clothes and be ready by the third day, because on that day the Lord will come down on Mount Sinai in the sight of all the people.'" **Exodus 19:10-11 NIV**

All of Israel was invited to be with God on the mountain, but only Moses and Aaron went. This passage goes on to detail specific instructions God requested about the meeting that she decided were too complicated. It pains me that she repeatedly rejected the opportunity to know God deeper, and I believe this is part of why she wandered so long in the desert.

Then there was the biggest red flag of them all, her continual need for idol worship. On a separate occasion when Moses was in the presence of God on her behalf, she melted down gold to create a calf to worship.

This was more disturbing than her missing the shining flamboyance of Egypt. This was her wasting the provision of God. Where did she get that gold? It was provided for her by God as she plundered Egypt on the way out. It was His recompense for four hundred years of wealth she had missed out on creating. And she chose to make it into a pagan idol? The audacity is shocking.

Between you and me, I don't think her journey was ever going to take eleven days. There was a lot of work to do. God was working overtime to renew Israel's mind, and that is not a fast process. I am, however, entirely convinced it was not supposed to take forty years. So what went wrong?

Like Israel, our battle *to* our promise is a process of growth. Liken it to the transformation a butterfly undergoes, if you will. The caterpillar enters the cocoon (battle number two) and every part of the former being is broken down until all that is left is a mush of DNA. Only when it is stripped down to the very essence of who that caterpillar once was can the butterfly begin to emerge.

In the battle *to* our promise, you and I are losing who we once were. Every part of us that will not serve God's purpose where we are going gets lovingly beat down, broken off, and pulverized until all that is left of us is the core of who we are. Then, and only then, does the new you begin to grow.

Sounds extreme, right? This is why so many are lost on this battlefield. You cannot endure this level of pruning without a connection to Jesus. The whole battle is designed to require you to rely on God to make it through.

It is His love that accomplishes this radical transformation. It is His battle to win on your behalf. You actually cannot win it on your own. The longer you stay at arms length from God the longer it will take you to win.

I believe this battle lasts between one to three years for those who are actively working with the Lord. Don't quote me on that because God can do anything He wants, but the patterns I have studied suggest that as a typical time frame.

This does not mean you are not bearing fruit during that time, or that your life always feels bad until it's over. It means that God is actively providing all kinds of opportunities for you to grow.

This can look like pruning the good fruit of your life, times of deliverance, inner healing, studying scripture, learning a new skill set, and so much more.

Expect God to provide for you in all kinds of distinct and

supernatural ways as He invites you closer to His heart.

Israel's story would have gone so differently if she had opened herself to learn God's way more quickly. She had been apart from Him for four hundred years. Although she knew of God, she really did not know God.

Perhaps the biggest misstep she made in the desert was her downright refusal to see her world through God's perspective. All those months eating miraculous manna, and observing God's presence descending on Mt. Sinai did not change her outlook on life.

When Moses was tasked with sending twelve spies to scout out the promised land he never dreamed that their report would become so impactful. I have to believe he would have picked some other guys if he knew the way their report would alter the course of history.

This story, found in Numbers 13, teaches us how important it is to listen to the right people. **Don't share your promise with just anybody.** Some people are not able to see life from God's point of view, and that can sow seeds of doubt you don't have time for.

Moses had to have thought he made a good choice in those twelve. After all, he also put Joshua and Caleb on the list. The other ten, however, were total duds. The ten freaked out when they got to the promised land. Spiritual amnesia took over their minds, and they completely forgot about all the miraculous, powerful things God had been demonstrating in their midst.

When Israel heard the ten's thoughts on the promised land she caved. These guys could only see what they were not. They could not see who they were becoming with God in their midst. When Israel came into agreement with this perspective her fate was sealed.

She shrunk back in fear unable to trust God fully. Shockingly, that did not send Him away. He kept working to reveal Himself, His heart, and His trustworthiness until she was ready to receive it. For her, it took over forty years. **How long will it take for you?**

God sent her wandering back and forth across that desert, which is smaller than you think. She had to know she was walking in circles. But with every turn she changed. She learned. She grew.

The battle *to* the promise is where we leave fear behind.

To arrive at our promise land we cannot be afraid of God, and we shouldn't be afraid of anything else. There may be giants in the land we are going to, but that doesn't mean we are doomed to fail.

Fear has this tricky way of convincing us the thing we are afraid of is more powerful than it is. Fear is the enemy's favorite tool, and for good reason. He doesn't have to be more strong than us, he just has to make us think he is.

I have always been a little offended when people have pointed out various fears in my life. Sure, the common fear of heights, snakes, or murders is one thing. I'm not sure I am letting go of those anytime soon. The real fears that God has an issue with are the ones that keep us from truly trusting in Him.

He draws a line in the sand on this battlefield. **These fears will be dangerous in your promise land because they are opportunities to comprise your promise.** They are open doors to give away what has been entrusted to us. They have to stay behind before we cross over into the promise.

Israel was so unwilling to address this that God had to adjust His plan to account for everyone but Joshua dying before they got their promise. This is how serious God is about the promises He makes. Remember, it's not a just good idea, it's a vow. He loves you too much to deliver on His word while there are still blaring red flags in you.

The more you allow the expansion mandate to take root in your life the more fear you have to let go of. Your promise land is amazing, but it is currently occupied by someone, or something else. You and God are going to have to dislodge that before you can fully enjoy it.

THE BATTLE TO THE PROMISE

Another significant aspect of your battle *to* your promise involves receiving the details. Quickly after arriving in the desert, God began to bring new structure, order, and boundaries to Israel. He does the same with us.

Each new season we enter offers an opportunity for adjustments. This new landscape you find yourself in has a different set of rules than the last one. I am not implying that some things that were sins are not sins anymore. I am suggesting the way we spend our time, the podcasts we listen to, the people who influence us, and so on need to be re-evaluated.

So many times I have been in this stage God will speak to me about this. Certain TV shows suddenly are off limits that previously weren't an issue. Pastors I enjoyed listening to are now not helpful for the next leg of the journey. Simply put, give God space to redefine what He wants to.

This leg of your journey is about learning the new you. The you you are becoming. The you He knows you to be. There is no way around this but through it. However, if you go through it with Jesus it is the most delightful and inspiring season!

One of the primary challenges of this battle is the war we wage in our minds. We will spend so much time renewing our thinking on this battlefield. Because if we had the right thinking to begin with, we wouldn't have had this battle at all. God is amazing at showing us which perspectives are not accurate, what beliefs are limiting us, and what to do about it.

When you emerge from this battle victorious you will feel secure, strong, and capable in Christ. You will feel empowered and filled with vision for where God is taking you. You will feel excited about the adventure ahead. If you aren't feeling these things yet, there is probably more work to do.

Don't despise it. Embrace it. Embrace it knowing your promise awaits you. Embrace it believing that God has entered into a contract with you where He will do what He said He will do.

All too often we are not waiting on God, He is waiting on us to let Him do what He wants to do in our lives. There is a lot at stake here. There are people waiting on the other side of your promise who need your testimony to have the courage to pursue their own.

There is freedom for you as well. Will you make your bed and lay down eleven days away from your promise? Or will you rise and fight to become who God says you are?

Below is a list of things that can delay and prolong the battle *to* your promise:

- Constantly wanting to go "back" to the season before
- Complaining, and negativity
- Feeling stuck and immobilized
- Withdrawing from God/ not spending time with Him
- Refusing to renew our mind

It is important to note that grieving a previous season is normal and natural. Change can be hard…really hard. However, there is a line we can cross in our longing for yesterday. That line is when we begin to gaslight ourselves and insist on looking back only through rose-colored glasses.

When the past becomes the glory days we have missed the leading of the Holy Spirit. This feeling suggests that God did not come with you into this new season. It suggests that you are somehow experiencing less of Him now than you were before. The truth is that He is changing you, and how you engage with Him may need to change as well.

The fresh bread of your life is not yesterday's manna where God met you in a specific way. The fresh bread is whatever He is serving you today. The transformation that comes from this battle molds you into a great follower of Jesus. Look to be led in new and fresh ways.

Remember He is the one who brought you to this place. He is with you here just as much, if not more, than He was with you then. Whether it takes you four months or forty years, when you become who God says you are you will win this battle. You will emerge victorious! He will do everything He can to make sure of that.

When God finally brought Israel out of this battle she was nothing like she was when she entered that desert. She was strong, capable, and focused. She was hopeful. This time she had substance in that hope.

> **She had learned who her God was,
> and she trusted Him completely.**

I assume Israel thought her path was smooth sailing. The hard work was finally behind her, or was it? What awaited her was treacherous, dangerous, and strong, but now she was stronger!

She headed into the third battle committed, with her eyes on the prize of the promise. When you emerge victorious from your battle *to* your promise you will too!

CHAPTER FIVE
THE BATTLE *AT* THE PROMISE

5

The Battle *AT* The Promise

In 2007 I was in the Middle East five months pregnant with my firstborn. We were spending a month with some missionaries helping them build relationships to share the gospel. During a fun outing, we went to Petra in Jordan. It was incredible to see the detail carved into those cliffs.

However, my research on the 2007 version of the internet left out some vital pieces of information. It didn't tell me that it would take about a mile of walking just to enter the grounds at Petra before we would see the first sight. After that, we would be walking and hiking up cliffs for hours. Some of the hikes in Petra are multi-day hikes, if my memory serves me right. It is a huge area.

I was young, fit, and completely oblivious to the way this day trip would affect my growing body. By the end of the day, seven miles deeper into the desert, I was feeling super pregnant. Everything was hurting. My ligaments, my hips, my feet, you name it.

Exhausted, we finally made it back around to the first structure. My husband and I looked at each other, looked at that mile-long road to get out of Petra, looked back at each other, and then started laughing. It was one of those laugh-or-you-will-cry kind of moments. **There was no way out but the long way.**

There is not much worse than coming to the end of a very long journey only to find there is so much more road to travel. This is exactly how I felt the last time I found myself in the battle *at* the promise.

> **The moment we step onto this third battlefield is the moment everything changes.**

Yes, you are stronger now. Yes, you have more history with God. Thankfully that makes trusting Him a little more effortless. But you are also vulnerable. You are so close to the promise it feels like you're already there sometimes. Other times you are painfully aware it is just out of reach.

The battle *at* the promise is the defining moment of your journey. Everything has been leading up to this. All the preparation, the time, the energy, and the lessons are coming together for this Heavenly showdown. It was no different for Israel.

We continue our journey with Israel by skipping ahead about forty years on her timeline. We last saw her victorious, transformed, and ready to cross over. You can read this part of the story in Joshua 3-4. Moses had just handed the baton to Joshua as the new leader of the people.

The first of many full-circle moments unfolds as Joshua sends out another set of spies for a new report of the promised land. This time they come back with great news. Finally, she was ready to take what was rightfully hers. God was positioning her for a victory.

There was only one problem. She had to cross through the Jordan River, which was flooded from the rainy season. This river is typically between three to ten feet deep, and around ninety-five feet wide without the flooding.

With the flooding, the river was flowing with turbulent water that would have been very hard to get through safely. This is where the battle *at* Israel's promise provides us with incredible keys for our own breakthrough.

Here she found herself in another full-circle moment, just as we often will. Last time I checked, people did not have boats in the desert so Israel was in a bind. This river was standing between her and her promise just like the Red Sea stood between her and her freedom all those years ago.

This time, because of the prior victories, she did not shrink back from the challenge. This time the testimony of the past prophesied to her future. The weight of this moment called them to deeper consecration, and it will call you to the same.

Don't be surprised when you find yourself facing an oddly familiar obstacle as you battle *at* your promise.

One of two things is happening in full-circle moments like this. Either you are facing this challenge again because you did not defeat it the first time, or you are facing it again so God can show you the way you have grown since the last time.

The last time Isreal was pinned behind immovable water she was terrified. She eventually got across, but it was chaotic, scary, and traumatic. She really thought she was going to die. This time, pinned down by dangerous water again, she was confident. She was not afraid. There was no chaos because she was tuned in, and listening to the voice of her Father.

She was not the same girl she was before.

The enemy uses these full-circle moments to attack us with intimidation and fear. The struggle we remember from the last time can feel overwhelming and defeating.

The enemy's agenda is to get you to turn around because you don't know exactly how God will come through for you. But God wants you to attack this current challenge with all the faith you have now gained, calling on all of Heaven to support your victory.

When we find ourselves *at* the promise we will find ourselves in a holy moment.

It is a supernatural season where you should expect miracles, even when obstacles present themselves. Joshua sensed this and called Israel to a moment of reflection and consecration.

> "Joshua told the people, 'Consecrate yourselves, for tomorrow **the Lord will** do amazing things among you.'"
> **Joshua 3:5 NIV**

This consecration was a cleansing moment. Historically, when Israel would consecrate themselves, they would wash their clothes and abstain from sexual intercourse to prepare their bodies for what was to come.

The consecration was a time of undivided focus. It was a sober-minded understanding that God was moving on their behalf. It was a reminder that they could not do what they were about to do without Him doing what He was about to do.

At this moment, even Joshua did not fully understand what God was about to do. This is why you must be transformed in the battle *to* this moment. You might be here, *at* your promise, and still unsure of how God will clear the way for you. The old you, the one who had not already fought and won, could not do this with a peaceful, stress-free mind.

Remember, you won't be *in* your promise until you have become the kind of person who can carry that promise. If you are in the battle *at* your promise you are already becoming that kind of person. Take a deep breath, remember who it was that brought you all this way, and trust that He knows what He is doing.

God tells Joshua to command the ark of the covenant (the representation of God's presence in their midst), and twelve men to step into the Jordan River. As soon as they do the water begins to stop upstream. This is such a powerful full-circle moment for Israel!

THE BATTLE AT THE PROMISE

They all walked across the river on dry ground!

> "Yet as soon as the priests who carried the ark reached the Jordan **and their feet touched the water's edge,** the water from upstream stopped flowing. It piled up in a heap a great distance away." **Joshua 3:15-16 NIV**

This "great distance away" was a town called Adam, which was sixteen and three-quarter miles upstream. The amount of precision God utilized throughout this entire story was truly above and beyond. The moment their feet touched the water it stopped flowing nearly seventeen miles upstream.

Then, the moment they stepped out of the river bed the waters returned to their place. This was a masterful orchestration by the God who had vowed to bring them into their promise, and now was doing just that.

When you are *at* your promise you will need Him to utilize this same precision to open doors that only He can open, and He will do it. He did it for Israel, and He will do it for you!

Some may read this story and not fully grasp the reality of it. It does, I will admit, sound a little fantastical. If that is you, you should know that this exact same situation (where the Jordan River "piled up in a heap" in Adam) also happened in 1267 AD, 1906 AD, and 1927 AD. It is now recorded history.

Take a moment to envision this situation. You are waiting at this obstacle, unsure of how God is going to make a way for you to get across. God tells you to go stand in the water. Unusual, but you are willing. You stand there, and unbeknownst to you, the water immediately stops, only it is too far away for you to see.

You are waiting, obeying, and it very much seems like nothing is happening. From God's view, the plan is well on its way, the ball is rolling, and all the parts are in motion.

From your view your clothes are wet, the ark is heavy, and the water is still flowing. I would be wondering, *"How long am I supposed*

THE EXPANSION MANDATE

to stand here if nothing is happening?"

We have no idea how long it took for the water to dry up. We only know the miracle was immediately evident to the people seventeen miles upstream.

At an average walking pace, you would need five to six hours to get to Adam to see the water stopped for yourself. This was not visible to their natural eyes. We also have to assume it was not instantly dry ground.

All of us will face a similar moment of foolish uncertainty when we are standing *at* our promise. *"What am I doing? Why did I think I could do this?"* become familiar thoughts. In your battle *at* the promise, the enemy will throw everything he can at you.

The enemy will try to get you to doubt. He will try to get you to quit. He will try to hurt you so you aren't strong enough to stay standing as you wait. He knows he's toast as soon as you get across, so while you are still crossing he will keep coming at you full speed.

The battle *at* the promise requires courage. It is impossible to win it without courage. Even Israel could not do it without courage. This is why Joshua received a commissioning of courage as he became Israel's leader. You will also need tremendous courage to win.

However, courage is not the only thing you need to win. The hardest part of this battle is patience. Patience is the unsung hero of promise-carrying. Patience is not distracting ourselves so we don't notice the time passing by. Patience is not wavering in trust as the time passes by.

How long would it take for the water to dry up? Israel didn't know, and I don't think she cared. She knew He would do it. She prepared for it. She consecrated herself for it. Now she waited for it.

In your battle *at* your promise you will have a choice to make: stand and wait, or quit.

THE BATTLE AT THE PROMISE

Wait for God to do the amazing thing He vowed He would do, or decide it is not worth it. This should be an easy decision. How could it not be worth it? How could you come this far and turn around now? Why allow fear, intimidation, and the enemy's schemes to send you back to the desert?

You can't. You must stand there wet, tired, and patient because **He has already set your crossing in motion.** The moment you put your feet in that metaphorical river it was done. Mission accomplished. To give up now would be to forfeit everything.

In your battle *at* the promise, there will be moments of intensity, where it seems like this promise absolutely will not be happening. Then it will happen. Just like that the ground will dry up, and you will have to move.

You can't stay in this battle. You have to cross towards your promise or you'll be forced by the rising water back toward your desert. Thankfully, this battle doesn't last very long.

One of my favorite parts of this story is in Joshua 4:4-9. Joshua tells the twelve men (who represent each of the twelve tribes of Israel) to pick up a stone from the dry river bed. They take the twelve big rocks and create a memorial on the promised side of the river.

God wanted this memorial to be something they could bring their children and grandchildren to. A place that would remind them of God's miraculous ability to fulfill His promises.

The expansion mandate is ultimately about your legacy. Those who will come after you will be living in blessing because you fought and won. They will stand on your shoulders and what seemed impossible to you will be probable to them.

This is the power of testimony. This is why you fight. This is why you stand soggy and uncertain waiting for your breakthrough.

God cares about you and He cares about your legacy. Victory is as much about the people who are coming behind you as it is for you directly.

Never hesitate to remind your children about the wonderful things God has done on your expansion journey. Take a memento from your crossing and display it for all your house to see.

As Israel crossed over on dry ground she finally crossed into her promise. But there was one final battle awaiting her, and this one was the most important of all.

CHAPTER SIX
THE BATTLE *IN* THE PROMISE

6

The Battle *IN* The Promise

We are all tempted to live comfortably in the afterglow of a God victory. The greater the victory the greater the temptation to hang around yesterday a little while longer. For most people in Israel, crossing the Jordan was the pinnacle of life moment. Of all the miraculous things God had done for them, none were as significant as that.

They knew it, and everyone around them knew it too.

When we cross through our battle *at* our promise we must be careful to not make our victory a final destination. These victories we are experiencing are significant and powerful, but they are not the end in itself. We are called to expand and to keep expanding. When we shift our perspective onto thinking we are the great one, or that we somehow made this happen for God, we begin to shrink.

News of Israel's miracle spread quickly. How could it not? God ensured this when He stopped the water several towns away. Scholars believe that flood had impacted twenty-nine percent of the region!

Because of this, everyone knew of Israel's God, and His ability to open the water for His people.

She now had a powerful new reputation and a newfound fame. She could have easily settled by that river, forever being known as the one God dried the river for. Her ego would have loved that! She could remind every passerby of her special place in God's heart because of what He did for her, but her crossing was not for notoriety or fame. It was for a higher purpose.

The Jordan crossing was a right of passage. It was a visible shift in season, and it was a crossing into a new anointing. No longer was she wandering aimlessly, aware of her higher calling while being nowhere near it. Now she was standing *in* her promise. It was happening. It was finally happening!

The first few moments in this new land give us insight into the process God invites us into when we arrive at our promise. You can read the full story in Joshua 5. The first step *in* the promise was to circumcise all the men, which is not how I envisioned the story unfolding.

In the Old Testament, circumcision was the sign of covenant. All the men of God were required to undergo this procedure because this was how they demonstrated they belonged to God as the people of God. It was a physical sign marking them as God's children.

In the New Testament, the sign of covenant became water baptism instead of circumcision. Now all men and women are invited to demonstrate their sign of covenant belonging through water baptism. Now the sign that marked them as God's children was on their hearts.

While it may seem cruel to require all the men to immediately undergo this step it was necessary. Israel was being marked again as a people in covenant with God. Her forefathers had this mark and now it was her turn. She was signaling she was now a promise carrier. This was the time when she would truly begin to reflect the likeness of God to the people around her.

THE BATTLE IN THE PROMISE

After the collective circumcision, God gave Israel time to rest and heal. The second step *in* the promise was to celebrate Passover. This was yet another full-circle moment for Israel, this time with a new twist.

Every other Passover celebration was a remembering of how God parted the Red Sea for her parents. Now it felt personal as she also remembered how God parted the Jordan River for her. Little did she know that meal would mark the new season almost as dramatically as the circumcision did.

> "The day after the Passover, that very day, they ate some of the produce of the land: unleavened bread and roasted grain. **The manna stopped the day after they ate** this food from the land, and **there was no more manna** for the Israelites, but that year they ate the produce of Canaan." **Joshua 5:11-12 NIV**

The manna stopped appearing. Can you picture this? Your entire life you eat the same thing every single day. There is not a day that went by that this bread wafer did not appear on the ground in front of you, until this day. It must have been so surreal.

Israel was now *in* her promised land and the provision that used to sustain her had changed. God's kindness was becoming evident. All those years of going out to gather the manna suddenly carried a new meaning. She now clearly understood that God was preparing her for her promise all along.

He could have supernaturally sustained her all those years in the desert like He did for her clothes and shoes. He could have provided food that only needed to be eaten once a week so she didn't have to work so hard. But that would not have served her promise.

Canaan was filled with various foods and produce that needed to be cultivated, harvested, and prepared. She already had the rhythm of going out to gather food hardwired into her so she did not even miss a beat.

Our promise often comes with an upgrade of God's provision.

We will find ourselves with more options than ever before. We will find things that used to satisfy us are now either hard to come by, or no longer fulfill us. We will be forced to make our home in this promise, no matter how long it takes us to adjust.

You may be wondering why someone would not immediately love being *in* their promise, but only if you have not arrived in yours yet. People don't change immediately overnight. Crossing over shifts a lot of things around you, but you are still you. For some, acclimating to the new reality will take some time, and that is okay.

The third step of entering the promise land is to occupy that land and make it yours. Often this requires dislodging whatever has moved into that place in your absence.

I want to take a moment to elaborate on this uncomfortable concept. There is enough room in the kingdom of God for all of God's children to occupy their promises. The kingdom of God does not operate on a zero-sum, meaning if there are five slices of pie only five people can eat pie. We don't approach the idea of dislodging by thinking: *it's either me or them, and it's going to be me.*

Ephesians reminds us that our fight is not against other people, even those who are against God. Our fight is with the kingdom of darkness that is empowering those people. Because we are in Christ Jesus we have authority over that kingdom.

That may mean that actual people will be removed from specific positions of leadership as God puts you *in* your promise. It more likely means that you will be able to remove the power of the darkness in and around your promise land.

In Israel's story, all of Jericho was removed from the promised land. It was God's land to give and He gave it to her.

The battle *in* your promise is the battle to embody who you are as a promise carrier.

It is the fight to occupy all that God has given you. It is the journey of displaying God's goodness so everyone can taste and see that He

THE BATTLE IN THE PROMISE

is good through you.

So many people never make it to the promise land. Many others get there and fail to occupy the space fully. How will you stand *in* your promise?

If you do make it all the way *in* your promise you should prepare for a fight. Even *in* your promise, there are battles to win.

Calling the promise land a battlefield might feel like a stretch. Most of us have envisioned our promise land as a place where the living is easy. We don't want to think about battle once we are there because there is so much battle to get there.

Unfortunately, refusing to see the battle *in* your promise is the quickest way to miss the fullness of what God is giving to you.

To occupy means we take ownership. To occupy means we respect the place God has given to us. It means we steward it to the best of our ability. It means that we embody Him as much as we can.

In all our previous battles we faced enemies a little unsure if God was on our side. *In* our promise, we know He not only fights with us, but He fights for us. He goes ahead of us to prepare for our victory. This is exactly what He did for Israel.

Israel said goodbye to manna and hello to Jericho.

God gave Joshua an unusual battle strategy to defeat Jericho and it worked. Once again God established Himself as the supreme power on the Earth, and the best provider for His people. With Jericho destroyed, Israel was free to claim her territory; but not without a fight.

Israel's journey through Jericho was a journey to greater authority. *In* her promise she was bold. She was tough. She was not embarrassed by the favor on her life. She was not ashamed of the land God had given her. She was confident that she was carrying the promise of the Most High God.

THE EXPANSION MANDATE

Our promise comes with an upgrade in our authority. Just like Israel, we must rise into the promise carrier role. We must become confident that God is with us, and that it was Him who brought us here. We cannot be embarrassed by the favor we now have because we need it to fully occupy this new land.

As we step *in* we need to remember we are once again stepping into a battlefield. At the risk of sounding redundant, we need to expect it because the enemy loves to ambush us. We won't be *in* our promise until we have already become the kind of person who can carry that promise. Yet even though we have come so far, we are far from perfect.

Even though we didn't want to, we likely brought some of our issues into the promise land with us. These stowaways make us vulnerable to the enemy's schemes. He desperately wants to strip us of this new authority and anointing.

This battle can look like sudden feelings of unworthiness or imposter syndrome. Imposter syndrome is the feeling that you don't belong where you are, even though you have taken the necessary steps to be there.

This battle can also look like self-sabotage. Self-sabotage is so dangerous for believers. When we have not fully dealt with our fear, insecurity, and wounding we can subtly work to cancel the moves God makes on our behalf.

Another way the enemy ambushes us is through apathy. We feel so proud of how far we've come we don't see the point of going any further. People will make you feel guilty for occupying your promise because they chose to lie down in the desert. They don't want you to succeed because it makes them feel guilty that they gave up.

Be intentionally guarded around the apathetic people in your life. They will sing you their song of defeat as they try to lure you back to the desert with them. Put Kleenex in your ears if you have to because you have a new land to discover, and you are not going back.

THE BATTLE IN THE PROMISE

To truly occupy your promise you have to believe that it was God who brought you to this place. God gave you the victory. God gave you the favor. God gave you the influence. And God is giving you **more.**

The expansion mandate is about the ever-expanding kingdom of God. There is always more, even when you cannot imagine how much bigger your promise could become. We end our journey with Israel on that note. She has defeated Jericho and the entire promised land is before her.

Battle after battle, God helps her remove every enemy from her midst so she can enjoy this new land. Miracles break forth as God fights on her behalf, even defeating some enemies before she can fight them.

While Joshua was in charge God helped Israel defeat her enemies in thirteen different battles. God was committed to helping her expand her territory so she could occupy the entirety of her promise.

Why would God go to such great lengths to help Israel? Because He said He would. He promised this land to her. He vowed she would have it, and He took on the obligation to ensure it would be hers.

Israel's promise journey is so amazing to me. I can't quite wrap my head around the scope of it. God promised this land to Abraham over six hundred years before Abraham's descendants finally settled in it.

For hundreds of years, God stayed faithful to this promise. He kept it guarded in the heavens and He watched over it, and them. This was the land He set aside for *His* people. It was clearly important to Him.

We should take a moment to celebrate Israel's entrance into the promised land. We should take a moment to soak in the scope of the effort, attention to detail, and faithfulness of our God. We should toss some confetti in the air as we stand in awe of His kindness and His power.

THE EXPANSION MANDATE

God, we want to know you as a promise keeper in our own lives! Help us to trust that You are watching over your promises to us in the same way you watched over the ones you gave to Israel.

Israel's promised journey is not a fairy tale. It is not merely a great story. It is an invitation. In Christ, we are now the people of God. Why would He treat us any differently than He has always treated His people? Why would He withhold His help, His commitment, and His miracle power from us?

I do not believe He does. I believe we simply don't understand how to be His people. We have not understood how to partner with Him through these battles so we can experience His victories on our behalf.

God wants to bring you into the promise He has made to you.

If you don't yet know what that promise is, He wants to make a promise to you, and then bring you into it. It is a tale as old as time. He speaks, we hear, and He makes it happen. And when you consider all that He obligates Himself to, He asks for very little in return.

All of us want to receive a promise like this and enjoy it forever, right? We did not go through all this for nothing. We plan to live out the rest of our days in our promise.

That was Israel's plan too, but it did not quite work out that way for her. In the next chapter, we are going to discover what we can do to make sure we get to stay in our promise and pass it on to the next generation.

CHAPTER SEVEN
STAY IN THE PROMISE

7

Stay In The Promise

Every promise God makes is a promise He wants you to keep forever. This is why the process of the promise is a series of challenging battles. It breaks His heart to have to remove someone from their promise. He will do it, however, because walking out a promise without walking with Him is deadly.

Israel's journey in the generations after Joshua was rife with challenge after challenge. God was doing everything He could to inspire His people to stay loyal to Him, to stay close, and to stay in the actual land He had brought them into.

In the Old Testament, the kingdom of God was defined by the literal boundary lines of the promised land. You were either "in," or you were "out" of His kingdom depending on where you were geographically.

The times that Israel was banished from that land meant they were essentially removed from God's kingdom. Yes, they were still His people, but they were not under His rule and reign. When God would draw them back from their exile He would bring them back under His rule and reign. These geographical lines communicated their standing with God.

There were three basic modes Israel consistently lived in:

1. She was living in His kingdom land, doing what God wanted, living in protection, and experiencing God's blessing.

2. She was living in His kingdom land, but not doing life God's way resulting in challenge and struggle. God would then issue warnings and corrections to try and get her back on track.

3. She was exiled out of His kingdom land, living a hard life under someone else's cruel reign. All the warnings were ignored and she was left to reap the consequences of her actions.

In the New Testament, we discover the kingdom of God has expanded beyond geographical lines in the Middle East. Now the kingdom of God is where Jesus is, and Jesus is just about everywhere. Every person who accepts Jesus as Lord now has access to His kingdom.

This is a good place to note the depth of the power of the gospel. We experience so much more of God than Israel had access to. Our punishment for our disobedience no longer requires exile or death. It was put onto Jesus on the cross! We now have continual access to His rule and reign (which we call the kingdom of God).

When we are re-born we become a new creation with a new covenant. This new covenant comes with Jesus as our high priest and the Holy Spirit as our encourager, advocate, guide, and so much more. God, once again, has taken the obligation onto Himself for us. The Holy Spirit now lives inside of us to help steer us toward the right standing that Jesus has offered us through the cross.

This means we are no longer in danger of exile. God will not send us away as slaves in a foreign land to teach us a lesson. We are under the law of Grace. Thank you, Jesus!

But God, in His wisdom, has not exempted us from the consequences of our actions. These consequences look a lot different than the ones Israel experienced, but we are just as susceptible to missing the goal of our kingdom citizenship.

As I stated in the previous chapter, we must learn what it means to be God's people. Some denominations put too much emphasis on our actions, and others put too little. Somewhere in the middle is the balance of grace, love, and mercy where Jesus is. There is grace for your sin. There is help for your shortcomings. There are also consequences for a hard heart.

Only God can truly know the motives in a person's heart, and motives sure seem to matter to the Lord. When we begin to drift from the place of right standing we have begun to withdraw from His presence. God lovingly draws us back. He will encourage us, inspire us with scripture, send a word through a friend, and so on to reveal the state of our hearts.

When those invitations are ignored for a long time He will send conviction and warning to us. Are you already connecting this pattern to how He interacted with Israel? Where we see the primary difference in the New Covenant is what happens when the warnings are ignored.

God will assess the motive of your heart and either continue to extend grace or begin to allow you to experience the rule and reign of someone else's kingdom. This does not mean you lose your salvation. It does not mean you cannot talk to God, or hear His voice.

It means you can be physically in the same geographical place, and move from God's kingdom to the kingdom of darkness. I am not suggesting that means you are suddenly given over to demons. The kingdom of darkness includes the kingdom of the flesh, the kingdom of ego, and the kingdom of self as well.

When we understand that the kingdom of God is God's rule and reign on the earth we begin to understand so much more of the gospels. The New Testament talks a lot about people not entering the kingdom of God because of the various choices they make.

My personal opinion is that these scriptures are not talking about salvation. I believe when Jesus says certain actions will cause people to not inherit the kingdom of God He is alluding that they are not accessing Heaven on Earth.

They've been given over to a different realm of power. It is not about their salvation it is about their ability to access all the blessings of God's kingdom reign right here and now.

Jesus was illustrating the pattern Israel had followed for centuries. God's kingdom is where He is, and to be there with Him we must follow His way. You cannot have His kingdom's presence without His rule and reign.

In the Old Testament, when the people's actions made it clear they did not want His way they were removed from His literal kingdom of His geographical reign. In the New Testament, the boundary lines of His kingdom have been expanded to include all the Earth; but the pattern remains intact. If you do not want His way you won't have access to His presence and blessing.

When someone is temporarily removed from the full access of God's kingdom it is because they have chosen to ignore His word and His way for a very long time. And it is actually for their benefit. The blessing of God can be a heavy load to those trying to have it without having God. His blessing is Him, and it cannot be separated from His presence.

God's desire is for you to receive your promise, make it to your promise land, and live there for the rest of your days expanding your territory as He leads you. Your promised land is about communion with Him. Your promised land is nothing without Him in the center fueling every part of your life.

Do you know people whom God began to bless that eventually turned from the Lord? How many people receive some amazing promise and drift slowly into complacency?

This is surely why Christians struggle with the idea of prosperity so much. Most of the examples we have been exposed to are people who are walking in tremendous blessing, but the fire of God in their lives is barely a flicker.

The expansion mandate is the invitation to be different.

It is the invitation to receive expansive blessings and live out promises with a passion for Jesus front and center. It is the call to expand in a way that truly blesses others. God gives us a clear directive on the way to do this in Deuteronomy 8.

Every person who accepts the expansion mandate should study this chapter regularly. It is the direction of God on how to steward your promise. It is how we learn to stay in the promise without needing to be removed for our own good.

> "Be careful to follow every command I am giving you today, **so that you may live and increase and may enter and possess the land the Lord promised** on oath to your ancestors." **Deuteronomy 8:1 NIV**

This chapter begins with a strong command to be careful so that you may live in increase. Increase, expansion, and blessing are His heart for you if you are willing to follow Him and His way.

The next seventeen verses recount the story of God's faithfulness in leading Israel through the desert. It is powerful! Then God wraps it up with a double bombshell.

> "You may say to yourself, 'My power and the strength of my hands have produced this wealth for me.' **But remember the Lord your God, for it is He who gives you the ability** to produce wealth, and so confirms His covenant, which He swore to your ancestors, as it is today."
> **Deuteronomy 8:17-18 NIV**

God goes on to remind Israel they are nothing without Him. This is not a threat, nor is it manipulation. It is the truth. Every good thing Israel experienced was because God loved her and had promised it to her. To stay in our promise we must never forget who did the heavy lifting of our journey.

This is personally so poignant to me. In 2015 God called my husband to start a business. We were pastoring a church we had planted. Adding a business to the mix was not something we wanted. At the Holy Spirit's insistence, he got his real estate license and we began to experience tremendous favor. So much favor that it has brought us to tears more than a few times.

In 2017 we started a real estate brokerage and again began to experience incredible expansion. In the first five years of that business, our brokerage had sold nearly two billion dollars of real estate in a city where the average home price is around two to three hundred thousand dollars.

As we have walked out our expansion mandate there have been countless hours of late-night and weekend work. Hundreds of dinners have been interrupted by the needs of the business. Thousands of hours of meetings have occurred. There has never been a shortage of work.

There have been moments over the years where it has been tempting to attribute our success to all the hours we have put in. We could point to my husband's intuitive marketing abilities, or his personality as reasons for the accomplishments, but this would be a violation of Deuteronomy 8:17-18.

Having these verses as our guide brings us back to reality. We were a couple of nobodies pastoring a little church of about fifty people at the time. We only had a few friends. We had no connections. Everything, and I truly mean everything, we have received is from God. All our success, all the notoriety, and all the connections have come from Him.

It was God that gave us the strength to stay up on those late nights. It was God that gave us the grace for the interruptions. It was God that helped us find the right people for our team. It was God who gave us the marketing ideas. It was God who brought the business.

I hope this story helps illustrate the importance of that command to remember the Lord and His role in your promise. It is nearly all that He asks of us in return for our promise land. The final two verses of this chapter drop the second bombshell.

> "If you ever forget the Lord your God and follow other gods and worship and bow down to them, I testify against you today that you will surely be destroyed. Like the nations the Lord destroyed before you, so you will be destroyed for not obeying the Lord your God." **Deuteronomy 8:19-20 NIV**

I honestly hesitated to add this verse in here because it is so intense, but I sensed the Holy Spirit emphasizing the importance of it. If the promise was from God then it belongs to God. If the promise belongs to God it is His to give and His to take.

These verses must be looked at through the eyes of a loving Father who wants the best for you. A Father who knows the heavy burden blessing without a relationship becomes. To stay in our promise is to stay with Him because ultimately He is the promise.

Below are some signs of a wandering, forgetful heart:

- Beginning to take credit for the work God has done
- Feeling distant when you pray
- Saying thank you to the Lord but not meaning it
- Experimenting with ideas from other religions
- Listening to advice from ungodly successful people
- Dreaming of your future and not asking God to help you with it

What would you add to this list? I think we all need to learn to recognize these signs in ourselves. Remember, the Holy Spirit is committed to His job of guiding you back to the place of connection when you start to head in the wrong direction.

There is one more key we find in Israel's struggle to stay in her promise that is especially important for us.

It was her inability to remain battle-ready.

Every time she would come into a time of peace she would lay down her sword as if all the days of battle were behind her, but they never were.

CHAPTER EIGHT
STAY BATTLE-READY

8

Stay Battle-Ready

Whoever coined the phrase, "It's like riding a bike," had no idea what they were talking about. Last year I rode a bike for the first time in more than twenty years, and it was one of the most embarrassing moments of my life. As a child, I was an avid bike rider. I could ride with one hand, and even with no hands for a short distance.

I honestly thought riding the bike last year would be easy because everyone says the skill never goes away. Well let me tell you…it goes away! I was swerving all over the road. I had to stop more than a few times to "reset" myself. It was humiliating and hilarious. I will admit that I eventually did get settled into an acceptable rhythm, but I have rarely been on a bike since.

There are some things in life we spend so much time doing we cannot fathom forgetting how to do them. If you told me as a child that my adult self would struggle like that I would have laughed you off the playground.

The only way to ensure you maintain the ability to do a particular skill is to continually practice that skill. This is why the Army Reserves have semi-regular training days. **When the nation needs them they need to be able to step into Army mode effortlessly.**

This is why many industries require continuing education. It is why athletes practice in the off-season. Continual practice, as annoying as it is some days, is the only way to keep a skill sharp.

This is true practically, and it is true spiritually. If you are like me, you have practiced parts of your faith so much that you cannot imagine forgetting how important they are. Unfortunately, we do forget.

I spent more than ten years learning about and engaging in regular spiritual warfare. I am one of "those" people who seems to encounter spiritually dark people often. Because of this, I wanted to learn as much as I could. I had what I thought was a healthy fear of how powerful the enemy can be, and I wanted to protect myself.

For more than a decade I prayed warfare prayers nearly every day. I bound up, canceled, and rebuked the enemy in my prayers so much it was effortless. Eventually, I began to get a little off balance. I couldn't stop looking for what the enemy was doing in my life and the lives of the people around me. It became a bit of a fixation.

Around this time God invited me to have a new perspective. He began to teach me all kinds of stuff that brought so much more peace and rest into my life. That probably needs to be unpacked in a separate book, but the message was this: I had come to falsely believe my spiritual protection was found in my vast knowledge of how the enemy works, and not in the Holy Spirit's ability to help me.

All those years I was not battle-ready, I was in the battle. I was in the thick of it, spiritual swords flying all around me (metaphorically speaking). God thankfully led me off the battlefield and into a quiet backroom for a nice long nap. For several years I rested, and I learned the power of fighting from rest. It was amazing.

It was so amazing I forgot about those days of battle. They were long gone, and I enjoyed the fight-from-rest mode so much better than being on the battlefield. Imagine my surprise when I found myself back on a battlefield, but this time my rest strategy was not working.

I had missed an important principle of staying in the promise because I decided not to stay battle-ready. There I was having to clean the dust off my old sword, awkwardly trying to pray like I used to, and just wanting to go back to the couch for another nap.

In the kingdom of God, there are different seasons in life. Some seasons are like the fight of our life. We pray, fast, declare, and wage war on the ways the enemy is attacking us. In other seasons we rest, relax, and enjoy a time of peace. Both are equally important. We have to know how to enter the rest of God just as much as we have to remember how to swing the sword of truth.

How do we do this? We stay battle-ready. Being battle-ready does not mean we are always on the offensive, constantly looking for the next threat so we can take it out before it takes us out. Being battle-ready is remembering we are in a spiritual war. We are always in this war, even if it's our turn to nap on God's couch.

My personal belief is that God will allow us to fight battles here and there to make sure we keep our skills sharp. If we have entered the expansion mandate there will absolutely be future battles as He expands His kingdom through us. We need to be ready so we remember how to step into victory.

> "Be sober, well-balanced, and self-disciplined, be alert and cautious at all times. That enemy of yours, the devil, prowls around like a roaring lion, fiercely hungry, seeking someone to devour.
>
> **But resist him, be firm in your faith against his attack—** rooted, established, immovable, knowing that the same experiences of suffering are being experienced by your brothers and sisters throughout the world." **1 Peter 5:8-9 AMP**

Peter understood the importance of being battle-ready. One of his biggest failures happened because he wasn't. He was caught off guard when he denied Jesus three times, and it nearly cost him his role in the church.

He understood, and wanted you to understand, that the enemy wants to devour whoever and whatever he can. The implication in this passage is that he cannot devour those who understand the principles of being victorious.

To be battle-ready is not to be constantly afraid of what the enemy might do. It means we are not surprised when he makes his move. It is being prepared and being able to effortlessly wield our spiritual weapons whenever they are needed.

True warriors of God walk in deep levels of peace.

They carry tremendous love for people. They genuinely enjoy being in the presence of God. All of this makes them dangerous to the enemy because they know who God truly is. They know He is good. They know He is all-powerful. They know He will do anything for His kids. This is how they go about their lives, freely standing in their authority as God's children.

An important part of Israel's identity was to be a victorious warrior. If she was to reflect the Lord she would need to walk in the understanding that there is no higher power, no one more mighty, and no one above the Lord our God. He is at the top of everything. Whatever He says goes.

Isn't this what Jesus demonstrated for us? He would walk into rooms and demons would begin to reveal themselves. The truth of His supremacy is not up for debate in the heavens. Every single morsel of authority and power belongs the Jesus. Every part except your personal power of free will. Think about the implications of that.

Your battle readiness is the consistent awareness of these truths. Your battle readiness means when the enemy throws you a curve ball that knocks your front tooth out, you don't have to spend months trying to recover. It means you rise in your authority and remove every scrap of residue that attack tried to deposit in your life.

We are not meant to live a beat-down life void of victory, even though we often do. This is why we must learn to be battle-ready. This is why we have to fight and win some battles so we can continue to expand. This is why we learn the ways of God. His way always leads to victory!

Every time a generation of Israelites arose that had not been to battle God made sure to pick a fight with a neighboring enemy. He did this to teach them battle skills so they would stay battle-ready. He wanted them to feel comfortable in His ability to defeat any enemy that opposed Him or His people. If He did this for them could it be possible He still does this for us?

> **"I will no longer drive out before them any of the nations Joshua left** when he died. I will use them to test Israel and see whether they will keep the way of the Lord and walk in it as their ancestors did.
>
> **The Lord had allowed those nations to remain;** He did not drive them out at once by giving them into the hands of Joshua.
>
> These are the nations the Lord left to test all those Israelites who had not experienced any of the wars in Canaan **(He did this only to teach warfare to the descendants of the Israelites who had not had previous battle experience.)" Judges 2:21- 3:2 AMP**

This passage goes on to list by name the enemy armies that surrounded Israel. God allowed them to teach her how to step into her victorious identity. By my count, there were eight enemies left surrounding Israel. Eight opportunities for her to learn to fight with God. Eight moments to trust God with her life.

It is important to God that His people know how to fight, and that they know how to win because no one can defeat our God. I find it interesting that God could have given these enemies into Joshua's hands. After thirteen battle victories, these armies would have been no match for Joshua. What purpose would that have served for the legacy of Israel?

Leaving Israel surrounded by enemies might seem cruel and uncaring. It might seem that God was indifferent to her vulnerability as if she was so weak she needed protection. Or it might seem that God knew who she was. More importantly, God knew who He had vowed to be on her behalf. She was not weak or vulnerable. She was waiting to find out just how strong she truly was!

On my dad's side of the family, I am the first Christian. We have traced our lineage back to the late 1700s and every generation was Jewish. I assume that lineage traces back to Abraham. As the first believer in this family line, I have experienced a lot of interesting challenges and spiritual battles.

I have had to break off all kinds of generational gunk. I have had the honor of changing and redeeming an entire bloodline. Sure, it has come at a cost, but I would gladly pay it again and again for the honor of being the first one in.

My life is a door.

Closed behind me are hundreds of years of life without Jesus. Behind me are hundreds, maybe thousands, of years of life without His incredible mercy, and the overwhelmingly glorious help of the Holy Spirit. On the other side of the door are my kids, and the seed of my future legacy.

For at least two hundred-something years (as far back as we have record of) there have been generations of my ancestors who did not know how to battle. Generations that lived outside their promise, and the skills of battle readiness were none existent. It should not be this way.

God has faithfully taught me the skills of victorious battle. Some I learned from my mom's side of the family, but the bulk of my training has been meticulously overseen by Jesus.

At times I have felt like I was given an unfair share of enemies to overcome, but watching them fall one by one changed that for me. I was not disadvantaged because I had so much to learn. I am blessed because I have that much more experience watching God move on my behalf.

I am convinced God wants every generation to know the skills of victorious spiritual battle. I am convinced we should pass down these skills to our kids and grandkids. I am also convinced they will have their own battles to fight as they keep their skills sharp.

My story did not end in defeat. Every single battle I have fought as I learned the art of spiritual war I won with Jesus. Today, I write these pages as a battle-tested warrior who is committed to teaching her kids the same skills God has taught me.

We have to remember that the goal is not total peace in the absence of the enemy. **The goal is total victory despite the presence of the enemy.** As long as we are alive the enemy will be lurking just around the corner.

When Jesus comes back we can finally be in total peace with no threat. Before that time comes we have no other option but to stay battle-ready if we want to participate in the expansion mandate.

Our expansion mandate requires us to consider our legacy. It requires us to look beyond ourselves and into the next generation. How does our life inspire them? In what ways does our testimony give them strength to face their enemies? In what ways are we trying to fight their battles for them?

Joshua is a personal hero of mine. Out of millions of people in Israel, he and Caleb were the only ones to walk out of Egypt as slaves and into the promised land. Joshua died at one hundred and ten years old. He lived an amazing life filled with wild adventures, conquests, miracles, and promises fulfilled.

As much as we should celebrate Joshua with hero status there is also a troubling aspect of his legacy. The generation that followed Joshua rose up without knowing the Lord or what He had done for

Israel. How could this be? How could one of the greatest warriors and leaders of Israel have allowed this?

It seems to me they lost their understanding of battle readiness. While I do not know this for certain, I wonder if Joshua's generation was so good at battle they opted to also fight their kid's battles, rather than letting them learn to fight for themselves.

In the name of safety and protection, they robbed the future generation of the joy of knowing a God who not only fights alongside you but ensures you win.

As a mom, I feel this so deeply. I want to fight my kids' battles for them. After all, I know how to do it, and I do it pretty well. I tend to think, *"I can nip this attack in the bud because I have been there and done that!"* The only reason I don't is because of Joshua's legacy.

My kids need to know the God who fights with them and for them. They need to learn how to engage Him when they face a spiritual battle. I can, and do, share my wisdom from my victories, but I don't protect them from their opportunities to learn. There is just too much at stake if I do.

I want them to be battle-ready. No, I need them to be battle-ready. Our enemy is not going to stop coming. All the peace, blessing, and freedom my husband and I have learned to bring into our lives does not change the fact that the enemy is still prowling around them.

Ultimately, I do this because **I am completely confident that God will do for them what He has done for me.** There is nothing uniquely special about those of us who have a plethora of spiritual victories on our resume.

We are simply those who choose to keep going, to take God at His word, and learn to live in His way. We know God well enough to know He wants every single one of us to receive His promise, live it out well, and pass it on to those who will come after us.

CHAPTER NINE
NEW LEVEL, NEW YOU

9

New Level, New you

I have a confession to make, and I hope you hear me out before jumping to conclusions. I really dislike the phrase, "new levels, new devils." Phew. I said it. It feels good to get that off my chest.

In all seriousness, I would like to know where I can submit a request to have that phrase memory wiped from the body of Christ Men In Black style. This phrase has seeded fear in the hearts of so many people. It has caused us to shrink back in fear of what new devil might be lurking behind the corner of our next breakthrough.

I remember when I first started to learn this concept. I was fresh out of college and experiencing a lot of spiritual warfare for the first time. I'm talking night terrors and crazy paranormal kind of stuff. In my search for help from anyone who knew anything about this topic, I heard that phrase for the first time.

A kind soul "encouraged" me saying, "Rachel, I think your discernment gift is growing and that is why the enemy is attacking you. You're in a new level of gifting and you are now fighting new, stronger enemies. New levels equals new devils." Right then and there a seed of darkness was planted in my heart.

The problem with this ideology is twofold. First, it is entirely un-biblical. Second, it makes people afraid to grow in their faith. If having more faith means you will encounter stronger demons then I think I am fine with my mustard seed.

Why would I continue to level up if I will eventually have to square off with the top dog himself? I don't want to face Satan! If my every upgrade is met with a never-ending assault of demons, principalities, and everything else listed in Ephesians 6 I might as well stay right here.

This belief system is not biblical, and if you have it I truly feel for you. I lived with this belief for a very long time. It simultaneously comforted, and condemned me. Eventually, God began to whisper to me. That whisper sparked a dream for a day when I wouldn't be attacked by the enemy at all times. I realized Jesus died for us to have total victory over every single thing the enemy tries to do!

Biblically speaking, there are varying degrees of hierarchy in the kingdom of darkness. Paul mentions a few of them in Ephesians 6. While it is true that the so-called "higher" levels of power seem to reserve their attention for people making a larger kingdom impact, the amount of authority they have is still basically zero.

Jesus was given all authority in the heavens and the earth. All of it. Nothing is left for them. The only power they get is the power we give to the darkness by humoring their thoughts, following their ways, and believing in their false teachings. When we look with our human eyes that can seem like a lot of power.

I've spent some time in the Middle East and I can attest there is power there. Millions of people have given their God-given willpower to those powers of darkness, and that has strengthened them. I've been around people practicing witchcraft and there is power around them for the same reason.

But **what happens when people stop giving their power over to these dark rulers?** There might be a brief power struggle before the person is free, but then that dark ruler has less power in their possession. It is as simple as that.

What I am trying to describe to you is how limiting the "new levels, new devils" ideal is. Of course, I am not suggesting we don't fight spiritual battles. You are at the end of a book all about that. I am not suggesting you won't have moments where the enemy is raging at you and throwing everything he can to knock you down.

> **You do not have to fear what awaits you if you continue to trust God.**

In my opinion, there is a phrase that would serve the body of Christ so much better. Are you ready for it? **New level, new you.**

This is what I wish that kind person had said to me. I wish I could go back and tell my younger self that Jesus Christ, the ultimate Victor, was inside of me waiting to win that war on my behalf.

I wish I could have told myself that my fear of the enemy was enabling his power to be at work in my life. I wish I could have stopped that attack in it's tracks so it didn't last nearly four months. In the absence of a time machine, I want to tell those truths to you.

Will there be powers of darkness that come against you as you expand into your promise? Absolutely! But that is not the part to focus on. When we think about life in terms of the new devils we are about to encounter we put our focus on the enemy. When we put our focus on the enemy his power grows.

"New level, new you" calls us back to Heaven's reality. You are not the same you who went through that last battle. You are stronger, wiser, and more confident in your authority. Jesus made sure you became this new person before He moved you forward.

Let's break this down practically. You have advanced and have become stronger. You now know more about the ways of God's victory, which makes you dangerous to the enemy. The enemy wants to stop you so he will throw a curve ball at you. However, he has not advanced. He is at the same level of power he was to start with. Would it be fair to conclude this new power of darkness is not more powerful than the new you? Yes, it would.

Let's take it a step further. Every demon and power of darkness was on the earth the day Jesus was nailed to the cross. Every demonic power witnessed His Resurrection. They also witnessed His ascension to Heaven as He was seated at the right hand of the Father.

It is safe to say they know how powerful Jesus is. Are we to cower in fear of what the enemy might do? NO! He cowers in fear because that Jesus they watched dominate them now lives in you!!

God is inviting you, through the expansion mandate, to an ever-increasing life with Him.

Jesus has set you up for victory after victory. You will rise to new levels, and you will find a new you there. The new you will encounter challenging spiritual obstacles, but the new you will be stronger, more confident in your faith, and more ready to exact a swift victory.

When I started writing this book I was not sure I loved the idea of battle language. I do not want to give the impression that the process is too heavy, exhausting, filled with challenges, or lacking reward. I do not want to suggest violence either. Honestly, though, it is a battle.

It is hard to fight victoriously when we have limiting beliefs about who God is. It is a battle to transform our minds to the truth. It is hard to have courage when we don't know if God will come through. Of course, we know He can, but we don't always know He will. It is a battle to trust Him.

Obviously, I settled on battle language and imagery. I chose it for one specific purpose: this is more than just a process or a journey. There is an endpoint where you will shift into a new season with every battle victory.

Still, calling it a battle doesn't quite hit the mark of what I know to be true about this process. When we use war-like language it gives the impression that we are not sure of the outcome. When two countries go to war the victor is often undecided. But when we engage the enemy the outcome is always decided. Jesus wins every time, no contest.

The war between Heaven and Hell (when Lucifer was cast down) was nowhere near the kind of war we imagine. This was not a blockbuster epic story of two powers grappling for control over the world. It was more like a mean little mosquito trying to defeat a giant with its tiny stinger.

There was no power struggle.

Even today there is no power struggle. When we find ourselves facing an enemy we have to remember who is on our side. We have to remember who is within us. We have to remember who is fighting on our behalf! You are going to win when you fight alongside Jesus. You are going to be victorious.

God's kingdom is always expanding and we are invited to continually expand with it, even in our old age. The thirteen battles Joshua fought in the Promised Land happened after he was one hundred years old!

I have experienced so much expansion and increase in my life over the last twenty years. I cannot imagine a day when I no longer want to experience a new increase. I want all the new "levels" God has for me. I believe in this so much that I think my dying words will be prayers of increase over my family. Now that is how I want to leave this world!

A little over a year ago my Grandpa finished his race and went to meet Jesus face to face. Grandpa was ninety-three years old. He was a lifelong follower of Christ with a legacy the size of a set of encyclopedias.

My Grandpa was ready to go. I think he felt he had been on borrowed time for quite a while. After a horrible heart attack in the late 1990s that he should have killed him he had been ready to enter the glory of the Lord.

Witnessing the last few years of his life challenged my ideas of retirement, purpose, and so much more. Are we "done" in our old age, no longer having a purpose? I don't think so.

Throughout my grandpa's life, I observed that at some point **purpose and legacy become the same thing.** I am truly blessed to be a part of his legacy. Even his passing was a powerful reminder of the loving-kindness of God. His whole life was a testimony of God's faithfulness.

> **Every time we partner with the expansion mandate we make room for our legacy to thrive.**

That is what happened in my grandpa's life. When my mom (their daughter) decided to marry a Jewish man, my grandparents began a new expansion journey to make room for when my dad would enter God's kingdom. Clipping metaphorical goat hair year by year they faithfully prepared.

It took a few decades of preparation, but it happened just as God said it would. They never stopped praying. They never stopped believing. They never stopped loving. They never stopped sowing seeds.

I remember so many conversations with my grandparents about my dad's salvation when I was in high school. They taught me to keep believing, no matter what it looked like on the outside, because his soul was worth fighting for.

What would my life look like if they had decided they had expanded enough? What would eternity look like if they settled in their old age and quit sharing the gospel with him? I shudder at the thought.

However, there are a few reasons why someone would stop partnering with expansion.

1. They no longer see the need around them. They forget they were blessed to be a blessing to others. They forget that their expansion makes a way for other people to know Jesus. They forget God wants to use them to help others.

2. They see the need but they have been burned by trying to help others. The combination of ungrateful people and overextending themselves has left them so depleted they can't imagine handling anything more.

3. They are tired of the battle. They just want to live in peace and pretend the enemy can't get to them. They've received their blessing and they just want to live quietly in it. They are done staying battle ready.

I have known my fair share of people who have tapped out of the expansion mandate. They just can't bring themselves to believe any more than they do. They can't muster up the energy to even try. Church is a box they check off their to-do list. Prayer is a ritual and nothing more. They don't have any fight left in them, and it breaks my heart.

The hard truth is there is only one person who benefits from our rejection of the expansion mandate, and that is the enemy.

If you find yourself in one of those three categories I pray this is a wake-up call.

Please don't pretend you want to take up this mandate because you feel guilty that you are on that list. Pretending is the quickest way to die in the desert. My prayer is that you will be inspired by this book to go to the hard places and really connect with God there.

It might look like going to counseling. It might look like getting some deliverance. It certainly will require removing some lies you are likely believing. We have all been there, but this is the work on the battlefield that leads us to the victory.

If you take anything away from this book I hope you walk away knowing you have every opportunity for a promise like what Israel had. God has promised you great things. If you do not have your own promise yet borrow one from the over seven thousand He has already made in the Bible.

There is a new you emerging. Even now! A faith-filled, fired-up fighter is coming forth. A you that knows expansion is on its way. A you that wields your promises like weapons, entering your next battlefield with head held high, ready to receive God's victory!

Let these words of expansion inspire you to prepare. Treat them like the contracts they are. Expect God to fulfill His obligations because He always does. I am with you, and I am praying for you.

May all your promises be fulfilled!

CONCLUSION

One Final Note

As we come to the end of this book I want to leave you with a piece of advice. My heart's desire is that you would enter the fulfillment of your promise. However, if I may be so bold, I also know it won't happen for you unless you are able to grab the heart of these last few pages. They hold a final key to unlocking wisdom and understanding for your journey.

We are wired to want our promises to be fulfilled lightning-fast. These days, no one has time to waste growing goat hair day by day. We are people on a mission. We have a world to save! At least, that is what it feels like to me. Waiting, and longing for a promise is a special kind of horrible feeling.

It often feels confusing, disorienting, and aggravating. I wrote this book in hopes of peeling back the curtain a bit and showing what is happening behind the scenes as we wait. I want to encourage you to keep going. I want to bring some understanding. I want to light a fire in you as you become a promise carrier.

We cannot allow ourselves to believe we simply sit back, relax, and let God do all the work for us. We also must avoid thinking it is all up to us. The expansion mandate is a journey with Jesus. It has no real destination. There will not be an end credits scene after you step foot in your promise.

Our lives are ever unfolding in togetherness with our Lord until our final breath. This mindset was a hard one for me to settle into. There were years of my life where I truly believed God wanted me go make my own way in this world. Get-out-there-and-make-it-happen kind of stuff.

After that took me nowhere fast I swung to the other side of the pendulum. I quit dreaming altogether because I was convinced God was not interested in my ideas. I sat back, waiting on Him to do all the hard work for me, which also failed to bring me into my promise.

Eventually, the Holy Spirit brought me into the rhythm of Heaven. Somewhere between these two pendulums is a balancing flow of surrender and sacrifice. We surrender our will, our ideas, and our plans. We show up, do the work, and He yields the outcome.

True promise fulfillment requires acceptance of God's will, and His way. The "how" is just as important as the "what," and "when." I call it "true" promise fulfillment because humans are amazingly capable beings. We are able to do anything we set our mind to, but that does not mean God wants us to do it.

As I learned this for myself I discovered so many moments in the Bible that I had previously been blind to. In my Bible readings, I would focus on the fact that God upheld His word. I knew He would do what He said He would do.

It is all throughout scripture. However, now I know there is a missing piece of that equation. God will absolutely do exactly what He says He will do **exactly as He wants it done.**

Did you catch that? The "how" is an extremely important part of

ONE FINAL NOTE

the equation. If you want to see your promises fulfilled you will need to understand "how" God wants them fulfilled. His way is just as important as His will.

Look again at Abraham and Sarah's story. Abraham was promised many descendants. This couple was in their nineties and barren as barren can be; yet God promised a son.

After waiting for many years Sarah lost sight of the "how" of her promise.

She decided to get that promise fulfilled in a way that was common for barren women of the time. She gave her servant to her husband and asked him to sleep with her.

Abraham obliged, and Ishmael was born. Abraham had a son! Promise fulfilled! Or was it? God did not accept this solution to the problem. To God, the promise was not fulfilled because it was not fulfilled the way He wanted it done. They missed the "how" and it cost them greatly. This is an important reminder for all of us.

There are no shortcuts to our promise, because shortcuts rob God of the glory He intends to receive from you fulfilling His word over your life.

For Sarah, there was more to the story than watching Abraham become a father. God was so intent on displaying His greatness He orchestrated the first three generations of Israel's mothers to be barren. He wanted no misunderstandings that His people were a holy, chosen, and set apart people.

They were brought into this world through miraculous divine intervention as a sign to all people that God is a miracle-working God. To bring forth the people of God through any other means would pose a direct threat to His glory.

Make no mistake about it, how you fulfill that word is just as important as the word itself. Isaiah 55:8-13 also illustrates this so clearly.

> **"'For my thoughts are not your thoughts,** neither are your ways my ways,' declares the Lord. 'As the heavens are higher than the earth, so are my ways higher than your ways and my thoughts than your thoughts.
>
> As the rain and the snow come down from heaven, and do not return to it without watering the earth and making it bud and flourish, so that it yields seed for the sower and bread for the eater, **so is my word that goes out from my mouth:**
>
> **It will not return to me empty, but will accomplish what I desire and achieve the purpose for which I sent it.** You will go out in joy and be led forth in peace; **the mountains and hills will burst into song before you, and all the trees of the field will clap their hands.**
>
> Instead of the thorn bush will grow the juniper, and instead of briers, the myrtle will grow. **This will be for the Lord's renown, for an everlasting sign, that will endure forever.'"** Isaiah 55:8-13 AMP

I have spent years quoting, "The word of the Lord does not return void," and yet I often experienced the direct opposite. It wasn't until I looked deeper that I understood what this verse was actually saying.

The word of the Lord never returns void when it accomplishes the desire and purpose of God.

The word of the Lord cannot be separated from the desire of God, which is the reason He spoke it in the first place. The word invites us into a place of understanding His heart. The word of the Lord cannot be separated from the purpose of God, which is the function of that word. The purpose is how God wants the word to happen in our lives.

When we equally carry the "what" (the word itself), the "how" (the way it is to be done), and the "when" (God's timing) there is nothing that can stop the word from being fulfilled.

ONE FINAL NOTE

In this passage, we see the mountains and the trees responding to the word of God. They seem to be helping it come to pass because they know God is doing what He wants. **All of Heaven and Earth will come together to accomplish what God wants when it is being done how He wants it done.**

For many of us, we are still waiting on our promise because we have not surrendered our "how." We are still bargaining with God, hoping He will adjust the plan according to our preferences.

Drawing this type of line in the sand creates a great standoff in our lives. God's patience will far outlast us every time. He wants to fulfill His word to you, and He wants to fulfill it how He wants to fulfill it.

We play a vital role in the process as well. We must continue to offer our participation, even when it feels like a wasted effort. Sarah could not fulfill her promise by hoping alone. She had to try and keep trying for to get pregnant. Month after month for twenty-five years she had to present herself to her husband.

Even Israel had to walk through the riverbed. She had to get up everyday and remember the desert was not her home. Forty years later she had to continue to believe there was more for her.

What about you?
What do you need to do to partner with your promise?

We have to strike the balance between active participation and yielded surrender to carry our promise well. Some things can only be done by the Lord. Some doors will only open when He is ready to open them. No amount of banging will make them open for you.

Other parts of our promise are waiting for our participation. Don't make the mistake of assuming your promise does not require your participation.

Don't forget that God wants you in your promise more than you do! He is committed to helping you get there!

ABOUT THE AUTHOR

Rachel Wortman is an author, licensed pastor, and co-owner of a real estate empire.

Rachel and her husband, Grant, founded multiple real-estate companies including a real estate brokerage, Chamberlain Realty, LLC.

After spending nearly 2 decades in pastoral ministry, Rachel is now taking her ministry to the masses through faith coaching. She leads a community of leaders and entrepreneurs that help people impact the world around them through their faith.

Rachel is a prophetic voice, passionate strategist and bold leader. Her specialty is cultivating teams, environments, and atmospheres where people can grow, thrive and exceed their goals through Jesus Christ.

Rachel and Grant have 4 kids, and reside in Oklahoma City, Oklahoma.

Connect with Rachel

www.rachelwortman.com

Instagram @rachelwortman

TikTok @therachelwortman

ADDITIONAL TITLES

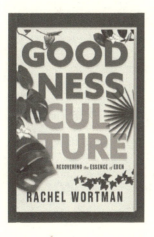

Goodness Culture

What would life be like if we lived from the foundation of the goodness of God?

In "Goodness Culture," you will discover the 4 core values from the Garden of Eden that we still have access to. You will also discover the 4 counterfeit values the kingdom of darkness seeks to establish in your life.

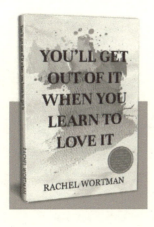

You'll Get Out Of It When You Learn To Love It

Through the lens of Rachel's previous heartache and burnout, she shares her heartfelt journey to embracing the abundant life. She gives practial, spiritual tools to help you do the same.